precious
bodily
fluids

a larrikin's memoir

Charles Waterstreet

review

First published in Australia and New Zealand in 1998
by Hodder Headline Australia Pty Ltd

First published in Great Britain in 1999
by REVIEW

An imprint of Headline Book Publishing

10 9 8 7 6 5 4 3 2 1

ISBN 0 7472 7375 8

Typeset by
Letterpart Limited, Reigate, Surrey

Printed and bound in Great Britain by
Clays Ltd, St Ives plc

Headline Book Publishing
A division of Hodder Headline PLC
338 Euston Road
London NW1 3BH

M102925/920 WAT

£9.99

GENERAL RIPPER: Captain, fluoridation of water is the most monstrously conceived and dangerous communist plot we have ever had to face. The fluorides . . . pollute our *precious bodily fluids*! They clog them, Captain! Our *precious bodily fluids* become thick and rancid.

Dr Strangelove
or How I Learned To Stop Worrying And Love The Bomb
from the screenplay by Peter George,
Stanley Kubrick and Terry Southern,
based on the book *Two Hours to Doom*
by Peter George

In all directions stretched the Great Australian Emptiness, in which the mind is the least of possessions, in which the rich man is the important man, in which the schoolmaster and the journalist rule what intellectual roost there is, in which beautiful youths and girls stare at life through blind blue eyes, in which human teeth fall like autumn leaves, the buttocks of cars grow hourly glassier, food means cake and steak, muscles prevail, and the march of material ugliness does not raise a quiver from the average nerves.

The Prodigal Son
Patrick White

A lovesong to my Mum and Dad

A sense of place,
a place of sense

In the early '60s my border home town of Albury lay flat on its back in the sun swatting flies in southern New South Wales with its feet sticking out across the Mighty Murray River into a part of Victoria we contemptuously called Wodonga. Every summer a photo appeared on the front page of the Border Morning Mail of a young lad in a T-shirt as striped as a bar code, with a freckled sister or two, crouching over an egg frying on a sizzling hot footpath, with the record heatwave recorded in three-figure Fahrenheit which still seems much more stifling than its equivalent in centigrade.

In winter the Mighty Murray would burst its banks under the weight of water released from the Hume Dam and householders up and down the

Murray River Valley would repair to relatives with all they could carry.

A drought would almost certainly follow. Bushfires raged and were doused by men and women with wet towels and blankets drenched with water from big buckets from Nail Can Hill to Monument Hill. The summer saw flies as big as frogs and frogs the size of small dogs. It was God's own. Dad reckoned if God came back, He'd settle in Albury, probably at our pub, in room 17.

In 1824 Hume and Hovell were the first white men to cross the river and they inscribed a tree each as a memorial to their feat. Regrettably a bullock driver accidentally burnt down Hume's tree and Hovell's died after they poured concrete into the trunk in order to preserve it. The City Council chose another tree nearby and got someone with good handwriting to inscribe it carefully with a replica of Hovell's markings. They built a wrought iron fence around it to keep sticky fingers from rubbing out the forgery. Tourists stood next to the tree and took each other's photographs with Box Brownies. We giggled at them as we ran down to swing off the big thick rope dangling from the huge branch of a river gum that almost swung us over the river to Wodonga flats. Aunt Faith said of the fake Hovell tree: A lie is the truth, if you believe it. That's the sort of thing that set me up for life.

Albury was called Bungambrewatah by the Aborigines but white men renamed it to save ink and bad spellers. In 1961 you could not believe it was once called Sleepy Hollow by passing travellers. On Saturday mornings you couldn't park in Dean Street and Dad and Mum, from their seats in the front of the Holden, would poke their arms out of the side windows, left and right, to indicate as we drove round and round the block.

Mates's store bulged with men's and women's clothes, furniture, toys, crockery, cutlery and something they called haberdashery. My theatrical cousin David aspired to be a window dresser at Mates. It was the Broadway of Albury. At Christmas they sprayed Santa Snow on the inside of the front windows which melted down like at the butcher's shop in the midday sun. The nativity window always attracted an enormous whirl of onlookers glancing over each other's shoulders to see if it had changed at all from the year before, or the year before that. In Mates's window Baby Jesus never grew old, swathed in swaddling clothes and Santa Snow.

The City Council was so concerned about the state of the traffic that parallel parking in Dean Street was introduced but after a time it was realised that it actually cut parking spaces by half. Traffic lights like in Sydney were discussed and discarded by Mayor Cleaver Bunton by tucking the folder in the drawer at the base of his chestnut Empire desk. Mayor Bunton neither drove a motor car nor frankly cared to. That was what Mrs Bunton was there for.

During the other cold war of the '50s, the real war between Fords and Holdens, Mayor Bunton opened the latest General Motors Holden show-room, Preston Motors, with the proud boast that he never handled anything more complicated than a fountain pen. In his firm sun-speckled hands Albury grew at half the rate of Wodonga. He had been mayor since the War but fell out of office when a worldwide sweep of pro-Catholic voting catapulted Kennedy to President of the United States and Alderman J.C. King to Mayor of Albury. From his Vatican balcony, Holy Roly Poly Jolly John XXIII, the other apple of all my aunties' eyes, introduced laughter into the liturgy, looking like a clean-shaven Father Christmas in white.

We all walked with a skip to St Pat's school – a Catholic President and Mayor! – but Alderman King was struck down by a fatal heart attack four weeks after the election. Not even the nursing nuns at the Sisters Without Mercy Hospital could save him. Aunt Faith variously blamed Cubans and Communists. Dad and I knew it was the shock and guilt of beating Bunton at his own game. Mayor Bunton was back in the saddle before the cortege left for the Catholic portion of Albury cemetery.

Menzies Bloody Credit Squeeze was putting everything out of reach except for glasses of beer served at Waterstreets Railway Commercial Hotel but it must be said that drunks were drinking less. That meant Dad had less money to give to the bookmakers around the local tracks who then couldn't build additions to the grand castles they built on the sides of Monument Hill where they lived side-by-side with life's other lottery winners. That meant builders and labourers had less money to buy beers. Albury's fragile economy was under the darkest threat since the War.

My father's side of the family had managed the pub closest to the Albury Railway Station since late last century and with it came a particular sense of loyalty to our State. Until the standard gauge line was built all rail traffic between Sydney and Melbourne had to stop at Albury. Nana Waterstreet called the standard gauge the greatest backward step this country had taken, adding that the States' identities were taken away and thereafter you could hardly tell a Victorian accent from a New South Welshman's. This backward step did affect turnover when 80 per cent of our customers – shunters and labourers – were sacked as superfluous and rail travellers no longer needed to stay in Albury overnight. It meant losing my good little earner for movie money: punching work cards on and off in the Bundy machine for railway workers while they stayed put in the bar. The supervisors weren't too fussed as long as I bundied their cards as well.

The Albury Railway Station was touted as having the longest platform in the Southern Hemisphere except for a couple in South America and half a dozen in Africa. It certainly was the finest railway station between Wagga Wagga and Myrtleford.

Just as we were reeling from Menzies Bloody Credit Squeeze, the standard gauge and King's suspicious death, the rabbits became immune to the myxomatosis. Boatloads of rabbits came over with the First Fleet and once they arrived in God's own they naturally bred like, well, like rabbits. They ate everything in sight but they were manna from heaven to a boy with a slug gun, a pocket full of slug boxes and the promise of 25 shillings a pair at Mackie's Butchers even without their fur. But the rabbits were declared vermin by the Pastures Protection Board, and the best minds in Albury came up with the idea of using a mosquito-borne virus that gave rabbits and no one else the flu. However, they also invented an antidote to give to domestic rabbits which was itself mosquito-borne and within a few generations – about a couple of weeks – rabbits were laughing their heads off at the myxomatosis. Farmers were up in arms as their grazing lands were nibbled away by myxo-toughened bunny rabbits.

The rabbit plague was always near the top of the news read out by Mayor Cleaver Bunton on 2AY, the Voice of the Lower Murray River Valley. He had the most beautiful speaking voice in the Murrumbidgee Irrigation Area. He always began with: This is Cleaver Bunton with the evening news. First he gave the footy scores from the local competition: Woomargama-Cookardinia 10 goals, 13 behinds, defeated Burrumbuttock 8 goals, 10 behinds, and so on through teams like Walbundrie, Tallangatta, Brockesby, Holbrook and Bungowannah. Towns too small to field a full team had to join with another nearby small town and become WallaWalla-WaggaWagga. During the local news Bunton referred to himself in the third person: Today Albury Mayor Cleaver E. Bunton opened the Spring Fête with an historic address.

In January of 1961 Albury was chosen as the number one evacuation site for people fleeing Sydney and Melbourne in the event of war. Local shopkeepers thinned by Menzies Bloody Credit Squeeze prayed for war. Yellow arrows were drawn in chalk on the blackboard by Brother Farrell following the irresistible path of the Red Chinese Communist army who were intent on invading Albury. The Russian army massed along the Berlin Wall in readiness. The army tanks from Bonegilla which clanked along Dean Street every Anzac Day causing cracks the size of river beds seemed hardly enough. Catholic boys prayed fiercely on their grassy-grazed knees against the inevitable show-down between us and them, between Australia and the combined weight of China and Russia, between Catholics and public dogs sitting on logs eating maggots out of frogs.

Spy rings were turning up everywhere. Communists plotted infinite ways to get under our beds. *Ben-Hur* was screening as a full-length feature after *Mein Kampf* at the Regent Theatre. Khrushchev had hurled two men into space and the Americans were still fumbling around with monkeys and dogs. The citizens of Albury were vigilant and ever-ready for the call when the latest world-wide Communist plot to weaken the minds of their town and make them more susceptible to indoctrination struck home.

It's not just the place you grow up in that leaves its mark on you, it's also the space. Things that happen to you when you're a kid may only show when you're a lot older. When I was just a toddler Mum and Dad were working behind the shop counter. In order to keep an eye on me through the front window they would either put me into a plastic harness with the lead tied to the verandah post on the footpath outside or put me in a wooden playpen with plastic round counters on one side tethered to the same post. Later as I was growing, whenever I got agitated or upset I'd work myself up into a great lather because I'd be torn between walking in six-foot ever-decreasing circles until I came to a dead halt or four-foot endless squares. As a result I was paralysed and stood still, too frightened to move.

One potato

The first time anyone ever asked to see my willie was in the back of Barry Stephens' father's green Humber Super Snipe. What for? I asked with a notion that the desired object was for more than peeing with. I was eleven. Barry was much older. He was thirteen. The thing had already been on my mind and in my hand for some time. In the shadows of utmost secrecy I discovered what no one could ever have dreamt possible. If you rubbed yourself up and down on the tartan cushion from the lounge placed carefully in front of Mum's three-dimensional swivelling make-up mirror you would get this incredible surge of well-being. On the one hand there seemed no reason to believe it was unholy but on the other hand there was no good reason to share this wonderful discovery. Some misgivings arose after several voyages of the self when moisture appeared on the cushion cloth. At first I thought it might be pale blood from too much of the rubbing. In any event it soon appeared that this magic gift had also been visited upon Barry who now wanted to do it. Together. Without the cushion, in the back seat of his Dad's car.

Mr Stephens had left us in the car while he retrieved some cartons of shotgun cartridges from the garage. We were supposed to go galah shooting. It was a sort of public service as they ate the farmers' seeds. How could you shoot those beautiful birds? queried Mum whenever I returned with a hessian bag of buckshot bird bodies. Sometimes they were large white sulphur-crested cockatoos or more often pink and grey galahs with the odd black crow, magpie or plover who happened to be sitting on the wrong tree at the wrong time. Magpies were a known danger to hatless golfers and plovers were furious darters on the football field if you were playing up the end where their nests were. Their wings were rumoured to be poisoned. So all in all we were protecting people as well as having a good time. So when Mum asked me that question, I cocked an imaginary shotgun to my shoulder and said, Like this, bang. There's nothing like getting up to no good and people believing you're not up to mischief but doing a good deed.

Barry had a head of jet red hair. We called him

Taillight. It grew elsewhere I saw when he flashed me, pulling his pants up and down quickly like a matador's cape. Curly red pubic hair like a rusty Steelo pad grew atop his uncut dick. I had seen an uncircumcised one before. My youngest brother Paul Damien was too ill at birth to have the operation and it just didn't get done for one reason or another. We called him the Hood. I was responsible for his being named Paul Damien and was really proud of it. Mum, Dad, Katherine Ann, John, Peter, myself and the yet unnamed baby were on our way to St Pat's for the baby's christening. Being good Catholics Mum and Dad had decided before he was born he was going to be called Mark and that was that. What they hadn't taken into account was him being born with two huge strawberry birthmarks the size of apples, one on his forehead and one on his stomach. It was with a wisdom far beyond my years that I pointed out the inappropriateness of the name on the way to the church. There was a sudden screeching of brakes while names were thrown around the two-toned pale blue and white with trim Holden. I chose Paul for purity and Damien because the Unchristian Brothers bewitched us with tales of his heroic toils among the lepers. I can't recall if it was a show of hands or on the voices but Paul Damien it was to be forever – or alternatively the Hood.

A blush the colour of a sunset overtook my

13

whole face. Then I could sense that Taillight saw my
embarrassment, so I blushed some more and I saw
that he could see it and the blush grew worse. And
so it went until I felt my whole body covered in all
the shades of red on a Taubmans paint card. All the
time I tried to keep a worldly grin on my deeply
shocked face. It must have turned him off because
he never asked me again.

Mr Stephens limped out of the driveway with a
cardboard box of shells resting on his hipbone, his
brown felt hat planted firmly on his head. No one
had ever seen him hatless including Mrs Stephens.
Neither parent had a speck of red in their hair we
could see and no one really knew where Taillight
came from. Mr Stephens was a bookmaker and Mrs
Stephens an addicted gambler when they met and
married in their middle age. Taillight became a lair,
people said. He later married an Aboriginal girl in
the Northern Territory and had a million kids. But
the year before I went to boarding school we were
the firmest of friends. We made gunpowder in the
shed at the back of the pub, blowing jam tins on to
the roof next door. We hunted rabbits for their meat
and fur, carried home dead snakes on sticks to scare
Dad who suffered the shakes from them, fished
with jaggers off the bridge for redfin and sprinkled
illegal aniseed oil from a boat tied to a dead tree at
the Weir, shot thousands of galahs who came from
all about to circle around us, so if you shot some

and they weren't dead after they hit the ground Taillight grabbed them by their claws and shook them like tambourines up and down. They were called squawkers and their screams brought flock upon flock of pink-bellied galahs that circled in a feathery tornado above our heads, thousands of them blacking out the sun as we banged away, falling two or three at a time in soft thuds to the ground. The squawkers' screams gave me the willies at night.

Even before I went to boarding school, when Taillight began to spend most Saturday afternoons under the bonnet of his car, we grew apart. He took to sticking his red hair with thick Brylcreem, while mine grew wild like weeds, unkempt, long and foppish. In short, he became a sort of frilled red Elvis and I, a stick Beatle. His later lairising cost him a little finger when he fell off a train he was shunting, the full use of his left leg when a bully cop on a motorbike ran over him on his pushbike, and then he got pneumonia after I visited him in hospital and gave him a box of peanuts and one fell into his lung instead of his stomach. I guess that was bad luck rather than bad behaviour. Anyway, he was a bad boy according to Mum while I was merely naughty. At the time it had the makings of mateship.

The back of the Humber reeked of Havelock pipe tobacco and polished leather. Mr Stephens was devoted to his car which he called the Pride of the

Fleet although he only had the one car. Taillight and I would get five shillings for cleaning it. Hose nozzles hadn't been invented or at least not in Albury, and you had to stick your finger over the end of the hose and turn the water up real high to get a decent pressure to wash away the bird shit from the bottle green duco – that's if Taillight hadn't choked the water by folding the hose like a broken stick. We had to be very particular with the Johnson's car wax and the Kiwi boot polish on the mud flaps. When we returned from a shooting trip the car looked like a red-bellied parrot from the dirt and dust.

Aunt Faith said I was a late developer. Some of the boys in my class almost had sideburns and faint moustaches. The closest I got to one was after a Choo-Choo bar. The Lebbo boys had hair growing like black moss on their legs and sprouting over their shirt collars. The area around my willie looked like Yul Brynner's head and nothing but nothing would grow from my legs, arms, underarms or cheeks. Not even down. I used a black pen once to draw a map of Tasmania on myself but it was a disaster and even the sandsoap wouldn't remove it. Aunt Faith said I was very young for my age which was strange because I always felt my age.

Taillight obviously took my knockback hard because it wasn't long before he was taking girls for a drive around the block when his father was out.

He must have cut an appealing picture to them with his perpetually shoeless feet with the caked black mud between the toes, his legs and arms as freckled as a dartboard and his face tawny where his freckles had joined hands with each other. This was not the stuff of my wet dreams then or to come. And so it was that I took the road less troubled.

Taillight was like one of those Fijian firewalkers. He could walk barefoot down Smollett Street to the Olympic pool on hot melting tar, walk through paddocks of bindii without blinking, tread on broken glass and not notice he was traipsing bloody footprints for days around the house. If I forgot my shoes, I'd have to seek out shady spots under trees and run like a spy on my tippytoes over grass or cooler concrete. Taillight called me tenderfoot. It took me a summer to get used to the pair of rubber thongs around my big toes. So I've always associated bare feet with manliness. I wore gumboots when shooting with the Stephenses, even in summer, what with tiger snakes pretending to be twigs and taipans rumoured to have crossed the Queensland border into New South Wales.

Still, we had the deadly fruit fly beaten with the Fruit Fly Block just over the Murray River Bridge on the way to Wodonga. But the fly is a slippery insect and can swim the Mighty Murray at night in a border cross. The Fruit Fly Block was set up with sentry boxes on both sides of the highway on the

Wodonga flats and big mechanical arms across the road to stop the fly. The scheme was such a resounding success that after a couple of years they only had one sentry box checking the traffic going one way. So the fly could go from Albury to Wodonga but not the other way round. Of course, they could always take the Barnawartha Bridge a mile downstream where there was no Block, which we did if we were carrying an Esky full of fruit and beer bottles going to the Weir.

After about twenty years the fly was defeated. The fruit fly is not an intelligent insect. Why didn't it just fly around the mechanical arm? Australians are generally a smart species. It only took forty years of collecting the road toll going both ways on the Sydney Harbour Bridge to work out that if you doubled the toll on traffic going one way and eradicated the toll the other way, you could collect the same money and halve the overheads and traffic hazards. The authorities must have been worried about people driving to the North Shore for free, staying there forever and avoiding the toll altogether.

Taillight put his forefinger to his lips when his father came to the driver's door where he coughed up the remnants of phlegm and specks of pipe ash from the back of his throat and deposited them in the gutter where they lay until the next rain washed them away with the entire population of Smollett

Street tadpoles. The raised forefinger to the lips is the international sign for mum's the word. You would have to be really dumb not to know that. I wasn't about to tell Mr Stephens what had happened. You never know, maybe it was genetic and he'd want to see my willie as well.

I grabbed a box of 12-gauge shells out of a carton and held them. Jesus, they felt great. Bright red with shiny brass casings and just the right thrilling weight. I don't know what it was but I loved holding full cartridges. Mums and women don't understand this stuff. Dangerous and beautiful and loading them into Mr Stephens' double-barrelled shotgun resting on my knees, too heavy to hold up to my shoulder like him, and clicking the gun back in readiness with my legs. After he'd shot, he'd break the gun in half and turn it over like a baby until the twin empty cartridges fell smoking to the ground, smelling of cracker night.

Taillight lived with his parents next door to our pub. Mr Stephens had three black Bakelite phones from which he took horse race and greyhound race bets written down in pencil on pieces of ruled paper on a school pad. Some bets would involve tens of pounds, straight out or each way, but mostly they were bets of a couple of bob. Taillight and I would boy the phones some Saturday afternoons if Mr Stephens was sick or away. Punters would be shocked to hear my unbroken voice asking how to spell their pick. More often than not the punters would just wander from our pub into Taillight's back door, let the flyscreen slam, place a bet and return.

From time to time the Flying Squad would come to town from Wagga Wagga or Sydney to stamp out this hideous practice of the placing of bets without giving the government some of it. They had to be called in because if the local sergeant tried to launch a secret raid, one of his constables would ring Mr Stephens and let him know before placing a bet himself on the nod. Sometimes he might actually be at Mr Stephens' but never in uniform. The police chiefs in Sydney and Wagga Wagga felt that the locals could not be trusted with the gambling and the licensing administration. Funny thing was, we still got a tip-off when the Flying Squad secretly came to town.

There never was much chance of dying of thirst at Waterstreets Hotel. My family had run it since Adam was a boy. The original building was red brick, square, and the size of a large shithouse but with the growth of the rail and more industries, pieces had been added like a Lego set until it finally resembled the Sphinx with a wrought iron verandah over its face. Like most pubs it was socially and sexually divided into the main bar for working men, club bar for the white collars with pens in their pockets and the Ladies Lounge where Dad's newly-laid black and white linoleum was stabbed to death during the stiletto heel craze in the late '50s. Sometimes, if there were children involved, the lady folk stayed in their cars parked outside with their kids and were served shandies and raspberry drinks from a silver tray. People seemed to know which bar they belonged to, who they would drink with and when they had had enough.

Dad had them all fooled for a long while when he chalked Free Beer Tomorrow on the counter lunch blackboard outside on the footpath. Everyone would come in and ask for the free beer and Dad would say that's tomorrow. They came back next day and it was still tomorrow. It took a couple of weeks before they all twigged but it got them in.

Mind you, there were some like Ernie Carpenter the shunter who had lost both his forearms, one when working pissed one night and forgetting to take his arm away from behind a train and the other years later when walking home across the rails. Ernie drank large schooners with his two hooks, handled as carefully as a scientist with radium. He never really knew when he had had enough and despite his lack of hands Dad would have to eject him when he was too far gone. One night Dad showed him out the front door only to see him re-enter by the side door at the laneway. Dad showed him out again, telling him to go home and get some shuteye. But Ernie was a determined little bugger and he staggered around to the back door of the pub. Dad was forced to leave the bar and confront him trying to get in the back gate. Go on, get out, bellowed Dad. Jesus, mate, cried Ernie, you work at a lot of pubs. His workmates at the railway called him Venus de Milo. Dad said Ernie should write his autobiography and call it *A Farewell to Arms*.

In the cellar Dad had a series of beer kegs hooked up with plastic tubes that fed into steel pipes leading to the beer taps in the main bar. Rumour had it that he had a keg of water down there diluting the beer but no one was ever game enough to confront him about it. They whispered about Murray River shandies behind his back. On delivery days the big wooden doors of the cellars were opened to the street. Men the size of mountains lowered 18-gallon kegs on thick ropes and hooks hand over hand down a slippery dip of smoothed planks into Dad's waiting arms. He tipped the kegs on their sides and swung them into place like they were one of us kids playing Around the World.

Dad wasn't your kissy-kissy type of dad, all over you like a rash. Although he was super-friendly he was a bit standoffish. In fact the closest we got to a hug was the Heimlich Manoeuvre he performed on me after one of the bones in Mrs

Westie's Friday fish dishes got stuck in my throat.

We lived upstairs in what was known as the flat. A coloured picture of Jesus pointing to His Sacred Heart greeted everyone who entered while a framed picture of a green Indonesian woman had pride of place over the fireplace in the lounge room. Katherine Ann had her own room and after the advent of the Hood, I also got my own room – out the back with the boarders. Room 17 had panoramic views of the beer garden which rock 'n' rolled on Friday and Saturday nights to the 45s and 78s I played from the record player through a loudspeaker mounted on a chair.

Two potato

Whenever I asked someone in class home for a lemon squash after school, they'd say they weren't allowed and their mum had told them that Waterstreets was a bloodhouse with the sawdust six inches thick on the floor to suck up the blood. That's when I learnt my invaluable sense of rumour. The things people say about you are almost always lies. There wasn't any sawdust because Dad hosed out the bars first thing in the morning and the water would take it away along with the previous evening's droppings of cigarettes, broken glass, pieces of shirts, bottle tops, dentures, newspapers and the occasional body part like an earlobe or fingertip out to the gutter. Surgery had not developed to a stage where parts could be reattached so it was all wastage and landed in the gutter.

After the smelly droppings of wet tobacco were flushed away, Dad laid wads of thick wax on the bottle-green linoleum covering the top of the curved bar and lifted the unbelievably heavy industrial floor polisher, that only he could handle, on to the bar and with one hand guided it across the swirling wax and around the curving cedar bar. The lino would brush up so new that you could almost see yourself in a colour matching many of the customers. Two heavy grey tills stood guard on either end of the bar, festooned with stick-on cigarette labels proclaiming the joys of the inhalation of Peter Stuyvesant, the international passport to smoking pleasure; Viscount, light up a Viscount; or Mum's favourite, Turf, the only honest indication of its ingredients.

Since Menzies Bloody Credit Squeeze and the inability of customers to resist pocketing the pub's thick glass Waterstreets-inscribed ashtrays as presents to the missus for coming home late, recycled wax-tin tops and bottoms were used as ashtrays. The stench from the night before gave up the fight after an hour of Dad's hosing, waxing and singing.

It was on mornings like this that I started serving behind the bar, learning to pull a beer with just the right size head, putting purple poison pills into the trays below the taps to stop reuse but mainly pouring port pick-me-ups for the early shift who drank them clutched in two shaking hands (except old Ernie) or with one end of a tea towel wrapped around the glass and held steadily in one hand and the other end around the back of their neck, which was then pulled carefully away from their body causing the glass to make its way to their mouth without too much spillage. Once they topped up it was business as usual. Their drinking was an art form. Too much led to the falling down and the throwing up. Too little to the shakes, stuttering and waking nightmares.

When the balance was just right Jimmy B, the yardman whose time in the sun made his face look like a thumbprint, and Dad would discuss world affairs from the Albury perspective. Fluoridation was on everybody's lips, but not for real because it seemed for one reason or another everyone was against it. Dad was against it for religious reasons. God had made water without this meagre ingredient and if he wanted to make it with fluoride he would have. Kids could eat an apple for their teeth. That's Nature's toothbrush. Jimmy B just didn't trust the politicians. How did they know the right amount? What if it rained and the Hume Weir filled up overnight? Or there was a drought and there was so much fluoride in the water you could walk on it? Like the Dead Sea, Dad piped in. Although he had done Latin not geography at school, he knew the waterways of the Middle East from his missal like the back of his hand.

There had been a ton of talk about fluoridation and those idiots in Sydney from the Department of Health had been pushing the Albury City Council to put the stuff in the water for years. There was an Albury Fluoridation Committee. Unfortunately for my teeth the mayor, Cleaver Bunton, was on the Anti-Fluoridation Committee and cunningly devised a method to stop fluoridation in its tracks. The town would have a referendum on the question. A referendum would both express and defeat the people's wishes at the same time. He knew what was best for his citizens and that a referendum gave them a chance to say No and perpetuate the illusion of self-government. Under Bunton it was himself-government. His political talents had kept him as mayor since the year dot although he couldn't even drive a car.

The funny thing was that the most vocal critics of fluoridation all had dentures. Dad and Jimmy B revved each other up with the fluoride question the way people do when they know a little about the smoke and nothing about the fire. It was still before 8 a.m. and the bar couldn't legally open its doors for two hours but a small crowd of shift workers had wandered in and after I served them a beer or two to level them, they joined in the great debate. No one was in favour of the fluoridation except the government which was probably why everyone was against it.

Behind closed doors Spike Cockburn, J-J-Jack S-S-Shiebs the live-in alcoholic pensioner and Jimmy B continued to rail against the poisoning of our waters. J-J-Jack S-S-Shiebs had lived out the back for more years than I can remember, at least eleven, and got a Totally Incapacitated Pension cheque every fortnight from a generous government. By pension day he had usually run up a decent tab with Dad so there wasn't much change left after taking out his board. As Jack was always a little the worse for wear, Dad used to sign his cheque for him before depositing it into the hotel bank account. A couple of years back, J-J-Jack S-S-Shiebs had an argument with Big Jeff Eames and left the pub and booked into Brady's Hotel down the road. When he went to cash his pension cheque at the bank they wouldn't accept it because they didn't recognise his signature. He had to come back to Waterstreets to get Dad to countersign it as Shiebs before they'd take it. He was soon back in room 6, with Dad taking care of his accounting facilities.

Dad loved to sing and broke into a tune at the drop of a hat. He started polishing the insides of the 7-ounce glasses called ponies with a red and white Waterstreets Hotel tea towel twisted into a great wick poked inside and singing, slowly and softly at first: Oh, oh, oh yes, I'm the great bartender, oh-h oh-h, bartending my way all around, and then building up speed and volume until the men stopped talking amongst themselves, stared at Dad and broke into a chorus of Oh, oh, oh, yes, he's the great bartender, bartending his way all around, But he bartends too much and he's lonely and looks like a clown, He's lonely and looks like a clown. Dad led them a merry dance most mornings and there was nothing better for a hangover than a song and a laugh and a double dark port and brandy.

Dad had the gift of the gab which got us the lucrative St Vincent de Paul contract after Menzies Bloody Credit Squeeze when, incredibly, even the great Menzies himself almost got the flick. Conditions forced the Church to close the St Vincent de Paul shelter and instead the homeless got a single night's voucher from Father Bongiorno at the Monastery which guaranteed a bed at Waterstreets and breakfast between 7.30 and 9 a.m. which they rarely made. In return, Dad got ten shillings from the Church which made him more than in front, even accounting for what Mum put on the plate on Sundays when she was well. Waterstreets was your home away from home for the homeless.

Most mornings the beneficiaries of charity were sound asleep in the back storeroom, passed out with empty bottles of methylated spirits in brown paper bags bought from Permewan Wright's Hardware the day before and half-filled Cottee's flavoured cordial bottles scattered between their legs. A hearty breakfast was not top priority. Dad reckoned he was on a good thing, although sometimes they pissed themselves and the stench would hang over the back stairs like a fog until the crack of noon when they rose.

It was one of Mum's bad days and when I crept upstairs and peeked around her door she was asleep, facing me, her face sad with something, her pale blue eyes hiding behind clenched eyelids looking anywhere but out. Her bad spells lasted weeks, months, but her good spells lately were only days when she was as busy as a bee as if making up for lost time.

When she got the bad spells she went by train or ambulance to hospitals as far away as Melbourne or Sydney for the nerves, with electric shock treatment, but inevitably the pills would crawl back into her bedside drawers and she'd start with beer only and then graduate over days to the Chateau Tanunda brandy which she'd hide from Dad and us amongst the Pine-O-Cleen and Ajax under the upstairs sink. We always knew where they were even when she forgot.

With Mum in bed I would have to run messages, usually to Florence's Chemist for the tablets, but I could do anything I wanted because it was school holidays until the next term which was my last at St Thomas Aquinas before going to boarding school in Sydney. Dad had gone up there during the War, doing the Leaving Certificate three times. He was too young to go to university, he said. I never thought he was dodging the draft because he was my hero, a sportsman able to swim the whole length of the Olympic pool under water, a drinker never drunk, a boxer breaking up fights with one hand and not spilling the beer in his other, a crooner singing into the wee small hours and waking a few hours later with the same song on his lips. When Greg Esler, a larrikin by any standard, told me that his mother said my Dad was a playboy, I puffed with pride.

My school results had recently taken a turn for the better and the Bishop Hensche Travelling Scholarship for Religious Knowledge guaranteed £50 assistance in school fees in Sydney. Boarding school brought little concern because I had no idea what it would be like but I knew I'd have to stop the bedwetting as I would share a dormitory with forty other boys who hadn't peed in their pants since they were two or three. Bedwetting and the rubbing were my precious secrets but only one needed the cure.

We'd tried all sorts of remedies. Setting the clock on the hour, every hour, during the night. Mum lined up eight clocks to ring on the hour to wake me up and remind me to piss but somehow between the fourth and fifth bells I woke in a lukewarm puddle. Dad spied an electric anti-bedwetting device in one of his men's magazines and had sent away for it to America. Doctor Mackenzie's bedsheet apparently zapped you in the middle of the night if any moisture touched the wires hidden under the flannelette sheet. I wasn't worried about it in winter but what about in summer when you sweat – and not to forget the rubbing! It would send Doctor Mackenzie's Miracle Bedsheet into a major firestorm. I was now so terrified of peeing that I ended up pooing in bed one night. Mum blamed the lemonade. Dad wanted to tie it in a knot at night.

The last Sunday of the school holidays had to be made to last like the longest day of the year. Mum was still sick so Dad made us dress in our school uniforms for Mass and skip breakfast because you couldn't eat from midnight before Communion. This rule became more flexible in time being cut down to an hour for solids and minutes for a drink. In time I think it would probably have been compulsory to eat before Communion but back then you'd still go to Hell if you had so much as an Iced Vo-Vo before Communion.

St Pat's was only three blocks away down Smollett Street but Dad took the Holden, three in the front, three in the back and Mum at home, and parked opposite the church at Shelley's Corner, next to the large green tarpaulin laid down on the footpath for the Sunday papers. Dad bought a pink Sporting Globe which he neatly folded into the shape of his daily missal to read during Mass. We usually sat up the back where he could nick out for a smoke during the lull. Sometimes he would nod off and wake up with a cough and reach for his Viscounts and almost light up before realising where he was. The plate came around twice on Sundays but he always put a folded note into it because I guess he was getting most of it back from the St Vincent de Paul; anyway he was paying for all of us.

Dad said publicans should sit up the back of the church because it was in the Gospels. The Pharisees sat up the front and thanked God they were not extortionists, adulterers, harlots or publicans. Jesus made a point of making friends with the lowest of Jerusalem society, the sinners and publicans. Maybe that was why no one would come around for a squash after school.

The priest spoke about the fluoridation question during his sermon but it was hard to tell which side he wanted you to back. He seemed to be sitting on the fence of his pulpit. It was one of the rare issues that Bishop Mannix from Melbourne didn't buy into.

The early Mass was best because your stomach would be bursting if you went to the ten o'clock but

Grandma Monahan and Grandpa Monahan, when he was alive, and Nana Waterstreet went to it because they'd sleep in on Sundays. They never sat with each other which was strange as they were kin but that was the way it was. Katherine Ann was going through her holy stage and prayed with her hands clasped together and fingers aligned pointing to heaven. The Hood, Peter and John fidgeted like ants. I offered to take them outside but Dad insisted he do it. It was for the smokes.

After church Dad lagged behind outside the back door lighting up a couple of Viscounts to catch up and talk of the race results with other holy punters while we hung around dying of hunger. Communion had only made the pangs worse. After an eternity we all piled back into the car while Dad picked up the rest of the Sunday papers including the Sunday Mirror which had photographs of topless women with black bands across their eyes. You'd think they'd be better placed across their tits. Dad curled the newspaper up in a roll and placed it in the side pocket of his coat while we grabbed the comics from the other papers. I'd read real slow to save something for breakfast. Even when I was a kid of six or seven I couldn't eat or even shit unless I was reading something and the best read was the Sunday comics while eating Mrs Westie's burnt bacon and eggs on toast.

We had late breakfast in the dining room with

the boarders who again had slept through Mass and had weepy eyes and runny noses, things caught in their throats and looked like they'd all seen ghosts. Saturday night was taken very seriously by the boarders at Waterstreets and Sunday mornings were particularly difficult as the bar couldn't open until midday. The licensing sergeant wouldn't turn his usual blind eye to Sunday trading if you opened before noon. The idea was it allowed the parishioners the opportunity to go to church and tend to family business. None of our boarders took the least advantage of this.

After Menzies Bloody Credit Squeeze, Dad had taken to using bedsheets as tablecloths in the dining room because they were a quarter the cost of laundering table linen at the Modern Steam Laundry. Dad cut more corners than Jack Brabham. This worked an economic miracle but the piss and cum stains put you off your breakfast a bit. Especially after some unscrupulous boarders began taking the cutlery off the dining room tables to their rooms and into their bags when they checked out. So Dad put chains on the knives and forks and spoons and nailed them to the table which certainly stopped the stealing but after a while the chain would break and Jimmy B would nail the next link to the table and the distance between the table and the cutlery got very small. You'd have to eat with your face next to the plate and your nose sticking into little clouds of cum stains and pick up occasional pubic hairs which even the Modern Steam Laundry couldn't disperse.

Sunday breakfast involved little conversation among the boarders and was a series of sounds of clearing noses and throats and moans and groans and the looking at watches or wrists where once they were before being hocked to check when the bar would be open. Eggs went uneaten, bacon curled and cracked and cups of tea with Sunshine powdered milk curdled. Dad read all three newspapers' racing roundups hoping that perhaps the results might be different in one of them. The horses were always getting beaten by a short half nose or left in the stalls and coming home too late. He'd bet with the big bookie, Doc Seaton, in the middle of town. Mr Stephens couldn't handle his biggest bets and besides, it wouldn't have been neighbourly. With Dad's punting Doc Seaton got a new car every year and Dad kept the Holden and Mr Stephens kept his Super Snipe.

Your mother's sleeping in, Dad said, so don't make a racket upstairs, play out the back. Mum sometimes slept in for months at a time so we hardly ever played upstairs and would climb up and down the giant walnut tree out the back and into the treehouse Jimmy B built one day on his day off. There wasn't anyone for me to really play with. Katherine Ann was four years younger with John,

Peter and the Hood each following a year later.

In a way I felt deeply responsible for their being on Earth. Mum and Dad had this Swedish Rhythm Method Counter that they kept in the drawer of Mum's side of the bed that was used to gauge the time of the month and whether it was fine to do it without getting pregnant. It was the size of a pillbox with two sets of numbers, one in black, one in red, going around in cylinders that clicked into place. I loved nothing better than hearing the clicking of the numbers into place but I'm afraid that I might have put Mum's figuring off since John through to the Hood were unplanned. I'm sure Dad just said, in bed on Sunday afternoons, look at the Swedish Rhythm Method Counter, the numbers are black so it's okay. It makes me kind of responsible for such a big family. John, Peter and the Hood are my children, in a way.

The Hood was out the back yard pulling a dead kitten we buried three days earlier around by its tail. Peter and John are too young for me and I certainly never wanted to play with Katherine Ann, a girl. We're supposed to go to Aunt Faith's for tea which is great because my best friend Tom, who's also a cousin, lives there and Aunt Faith makes as many pancakes as I can eat. It's really my home away from hotel.

Aunt and Uncle Faith live in North Albury in a green fibro home surrounded by hydrangea bushes that bloom in big round bunches of pink and blue. They have a Hills Hoist out the back which we use in summer as a tent pole for the tarpaulin that Uncle Faith had specially made, and Tom and I sleep out there under the starry summer sky talking of things deep into the night. Sometimes as late as 9.30.

Winter nights were spent with everyone playing cards on the green tartan blanket tossed over the Laminex kitchen table which was hauled into the lounge room in front of the two-bar heaters with red- and black-tinged plastic crinkled over a light bulb to mimic a coal fire and the sand-blasted glass doors closed with their reindeer frozen in mid-air. The cigarette smoke would rise to the ceiling and build up like a great chemical experiment while the Faiths, the Waterstreets, Uncle Jack and Aunt Irene and Mr and Mrs Guy would play deadly poker with unlit matches for stakes.

Three potato

I still had the day to kill and there were no pictures to go to because they wouldn't let you go to the Regent on Sundays or even buy fresh bread. Dad's special Sunday licence cost a couple of dozen bottles in the boot for each of the cops at Christmas in licensing fees. I often wondered why the Regent and the baker didn't give them a few tickets and some bread to open on Sundays. Dad, and Mum if she was feeling well, opened the back bar out on to the side of the pub at noon. There used to be a great sprawling garden there with itchy buffalo lawn and beds of different flowers, but Dad considered it too much trouble and money to look after and tore it up and put in green concrete to keep that tropical feel and to make the hosing down easier, with wooden boxes of gardenias filled to the brim with dirt,

cigarette butts and bottle tops. Sometimes I wandered up and helped serve behind the bar if there
was nothing better to do.

Television had come to Albury from the station
in Shepparton over 100 miles away but you needed
an aerial as high as the Eiffel Tower to receive the
signals. We didn't have a television set so late in the
afternoons Taillight and I would go up to the Hume
Weir Café in Dean Street, buy double malt, double
chocolate milk shakes made in aluminium containers with two straws each and take them over the
corner to Mates's front window and watch the
television that played even after the store closed at
five. The trouble was that the store didn't open on
Sundays and they didn't turn on the television in
the front window and watching the big grey dull
eye wasn't the same, even with a milkshake.

Watching television in Mates's window helped
me learn to lip read because they never turned the
volume on and you had to keep your wits about you
to know what was going on, especially during the
action scenes when Taillight and I would make the
sound for ourselves. Pchoooooooo. Bweeeeeeuuuu.
Pchiiiiiing. Pwaaaauuuu with puffy cheeks. Sometimes we'd mimic the newsreaders with our own
version of the news like: Mayor Bunton farted
today and blew down the Town Hall. We'd piss
ourselves laughing. It was better than the real thing.

Sundays seemed longer because there was never

anything to do, which, I suppose, was just as well because the last term of school was starting tomorrow. It was a lucky thing God said not to work or play on the Sabbath because sometimes it got so boring you actually really wanted to go to school the next day. That must have been part of His reasoning.

Mrs Stephens said Barry was up at the railway so I went up there to see if I could find him. She never called him Taillight. If she was mad at him for something she'd holler out his real name. Can you believe that Taillight was baptised Basil by his parents. He hated it. It made him really lose his temper if you called him Basil, so nobody but Mrs Stephens ever dared to. She did it less as he got older and stronger. Mostly she called him Barry, which was the closest corruption of his real name he allowed. Taillight was always up to no good, which is what I liked about him. He could be trusted to get into trouble one way or another.

The railway station was about fifty yards from our place at the end of the street. The station really put Albury on the map. All the shunters, railway workers, train guards, train drivers and conductors would drink at Waterstreets and it was a disaster when the Federal government conspired with the Victoria and New South Wales governments to put in a standard gauge between Melbourne and Sydney instead of each State having their own individual and proud of it gauge. We fought the good fight over States' rights and lost. Dad said he was determined to win the fluoride war. We were sick of being walked over and being pushed around. Mum said he wasn't influenced one iota by the impact of standard gauge on business but it was the principle of the thing. Dad's a man of principle but I'm a little more flexible.

Taillight leant over the pedestrian overpass that linked the nation and East Albury. It was great to ride bikes over and feel the bumps on your bum from the seat going down the steps. He had a handful of pebbles from the footpath and dropped them into the funnels of steam trains as they passed back and forth under the bridge, blackening us in big puffs of smoke. Get out of it, the coal shoveller would yell when he saw us. Once we plopped a house brick into the funnel and the train stopped and the driver got out and waved his gloved fist at our fast departing figures. You had to time the drop of the pebble just right to get it into the steam funnel otherwise it would hit the side and roll off with a tink.

It was spring so the docks which grew along the side of the tracks hadn't dried out yet. Dried docks made fantastic arrows if you put an inverted nail in one end and Scotchtaped it in. The bamboo that grew out the back of Batrouney's auction yard made great bows and Taillight had actually stuck an arrow into a magpie once which didn't die but flew off with the arrow stuck in it like flying fairy floss. Sometimes my bow string would go straight through the docks instead of slinging it through the air like Robin Hood.

When we tired of stoning the trains we went into the water drains under the railway that you could almost stand up in if you crouched down. They went for miles in all directions and there weren't pedestrian signs down there, and without a box of Redhead matches you could get well and truly lost. Taillight knew them like the back of his freckled hand. When it was time for lunch I asked Taillight home but he wasn't hungry and wanted to stay, so I left him under East Albury somewhere and went home alone.

It was late and Mrs Westie had left my Sunday roast dinner on the iron grill above the stove. The gravy was as wrinkled as Jimmy B's face but it smelt good with the mint she picked from the side of the laneway by the pub. Mrs Westie always picked the wild mint on Sundays for the lamb and it sure smelt like the heavens. Another good thing about being in a pub was that the lemonade flowed like the river and you were never short of a fizzy drink at mealtimes. My cousin Tom had to drink water with his meals. Red or green cordial was allowed only on feast days.

I finished off the lamb and uncurled the gravy

by mashing it into the pumpkin and two veg. Everyone else had eaten so I read the Sunday papers alone in the kitchen while eating. I'd check on Mum a bit later. After bread and butter pudding I wandered up to the back bar to see what was going on.

Mum lived in fear of police raids, especially from the Flying Squad who would sweep down on unsuspecting but forewarned Albury pubs in efforts to raise the government's stocks. Considering the afternoon shift at the railway and the woollen mills didn't finish until 11 p.m., the early closing time seemed very discriminatory to shift workers. There was nowhere else to drink after work, except at home, and who'd want to drink there. You'd wake up the kids. So Waterstreets opened later and earlier than the gazetted hours and also had two shifts on Sundays at lunch and tea. Mind you, in deference to the Lord's death there was only a single shift on Good Friday. We strictly followed the letter of our own laws.

As all of this was illegal, there had to be some wariness. The front doors of the pub were closed and the back bar opened on to the tropical cement patio with multi-coloured garden furniture and faded and torn beach umbrellas stuck in the middle of the tables. The Ladies Lounge was opened to men who preferred the indoors. Patrons spoke in hushed tones which sounded like the jet overpass on Anzac Day if there were over fifty persons drinking. There were a few loopholes in the law which Dad's legal eagle Harry Flood explained. You could serve a Sunday drink to bona fide travellers – persons who slept twenty-five miles away the night before. Their names had to be written in a book kept for that purpose with the address of the sleeping place the night before. Alternatively, if you had a meal, you could have a drink with it, even if you slept next door the night before. These laws were puzzling in their logic, but as Aunt Faith said, ours is not to reason why, ours is but to do and die.

The usual suspects listed in the beer garden smoking cigarettes and stubbing them into the tops of Johnson's wax tins used as ashtrays. It was indicative of the depth of the recession after Menzies Bloody Credit Squeeze when customers knocked off the wax tins to take home. G'day Chilla, said Dad from behind the bar. Would you give me a hand? So I ducked under the counter into the bar and grabbed a tea towel and tucked it into the front of my shorts and let it hang like a lap-lap. The crowd had collected into pockets of people distributed through the Ladies Lounge and across the beer garden.

Dad was talking to Mr Stephens who was standing by the bar on his one good leg with his brown felt hat pushed back on his head like one of those Jewish caps and showing a couple of strands of hair. They were discussing the race results and their general injustice to the punter.

Captain Jack Saunders (retired), who now worked as a clerk at the army barracks at Bonegilla, was sitting cross-legged in the beer garden, sunning himself over half a pony. He was a boarder upstairs who practised out-of-control drinking. When he got into the heavy stuff his accent would change into this pukka English style and he'd shout things like, Shoulder arms, attention, eyes left and fuck the Kaiser. He was given a job in the army office after being forced out of the regular army because of the drink. But when he was off beer he was a regular guy, very intelligent, who read books without pictures. His army training had taught Captain Jack Saunders (retired) to dress neatly and his greying sandy hair was set in place like concrete. When he was in the horrors his forehead would glisten with beads of sweat, in the middle of winter even, and his hands would shake like a divining stick over the Amazon River. He always treated me as an equal which probably wasn't much considering how others treated him and what he thought of himself.

Captain Jack Saunders (retired) asked me what I thought of the referendum. Frankly, I hadn't given it much thought, it being school holidays and all. But I told him that if it was as good as the Sydney people say, then the tooth fairies were going to be out of a job. Basically, on the fluoride issue the captain was in Dad's camp of naturalism and against anything that the government was for.

The trick to the pouring of beer from the tap was to raise and lower the glass at just the right time and angle so that it left about half an inch of froth at the top. Sometimes Dad would wink if it was an inch or more and say, That's my boy, that's where the profit is. The publican's profit. However, the problem was in trying to wrap my skinny fingers around two glasses at a time and get the heads just right. Dad and Big Jeff Eames, part-time barman, with Coke bottle black glasses mended with Band-aids on the hinges, could hold four glasses in one hand and fill them up with exactly half-inch heads. My boyish hands tended to tip one glass to the side so that the contents spilt from the lip continuously. Practice makes perfect, but I'd have to grow a bit more.

The hubbub of talk almost made me miss the ringing of the phone. It was one of those big black Bakelite phones with a steel cradle and a round shiny dialling face with finger holes that showed not only numbers but three letters of the alphabet. Consonants I think they were called. Waterstreets, I said into the mouthpiece. It was Aunt Hope from Nana Waterstreet's Pastoral Hotel in Townsend Street. The Black Maria has just left, she cried. Tell your Dad.

I didn't know who this Black Maria was but the tone of Aunt Hope's voice told me it was serious and it turns out it's slang for the police wagon and it's ten minutes from the Pastoral to Waterstreets with only two pubs in between. There had been no tip-off. It smells like the Flying Squad, murmured Dad, closing up the bar and shooing out the customers. Sometimes during alerts I kept cockatoo lookout on the corner and on a sighting would scamper up to Jimmy B who stood on the front step with a piece of string tied to the door which he pulled, bolting the door. Sundays being pretty unisexual with both men and women in the Ladies Lounge there were a few muffled squeals when Dad yelled Raid! and told them all to scram.

Everyone was running around like chooks with their heads cut off. Dad found the bona fide register and wrote in names and signed different signatures as quickly as he could. Thank God there was no forensic. Patrons shouted out names and fictitious addresses. Ladies ran into the dining room and opened the sideboard and grabbed aprons and put them on, pretending they were waitresses. For a time there were more waitresses than customers until Dad choreographed things a bit, sitting someone here and someone there in the dining room and getting Mrs Westie to put some leftovers on plates in front of people who seconds earlier were gulping down beers.

Before too long there were thirty or forty people sitting down in the dining room and ten waitresses and a dozen or so drinkers at the bar looking as bona fide as they could. Most of the local cops knew the locals and where they lived but the Flying Squad, coming from Sydney by cover of night, didn't. I was told to skedaddle upstairs because there would be hell to pay if I was busted before I went to boarding school, the child labour laws or something.

I took the stairs two at a time and went out on to the verandah to peek between the awnings to catch sight of the cops coming down Smollett Street. They didn't always raid every hotel. Just the ones that opened on Sundays. We suspected someone was talking out of school. It just wasn't fair, going after us all the time, Mum cried, just because we tried to support the working men and make a decent living. Nana opened on Sundays for thirty years and never got busted. Once the cops caught her selling bottles to someone on a Sunday morning and asked her why she was selling beer. Because they were thirsty, she said, and the cops left bewildered, without charging her.

My heart was beating up a storm. Weeks earlier, I'd overheard Mum talking to Dad while he was having a bog in the toilet. Not only were the banks killing us with interest rates and abolishing credit, but Dad had four marks against his licence which meant that unless he won the appeal he'd lose his liquor licence. Brady's Hotel down the street had done their licence and Mrs Brady's name miraculously appeared in gold lettering above the front door as licensee without losing a day's trading but Mum, in her condition, may not have withstood the demands of licenseeship. Five marks would be a disaster. Over and out. Mum's dream of a real home with a real garden and all might be closer but I don't think Dad could have supported us in the custom to which we were mannered in a real job.

I must have been pretty naïve in those days because the Flying Squad never came to the front door and while I was hiding behind the slim awning pole on the upstairs verandah the Black Maria pulled up across the backyard entrance, trapping all cars secretly parked out the back, and a blue column of running cops could be seen through the gauzed dining room windows running up the beer garden side of the pub. They must have jumped the back gate and unlocked it.

Mum sensed something was wrong and woke up. I went into her room. It was real dark, the heavy orange curtains were drawn. She asked what was going on. It's a sixth sense publicans get even if you only marry into the family. She said she couldn't go down looking like this. She flung the kangaroo-skin doona off her and leapt to her make-up mirror to put on a face that would meet the urgent crisis below. The best view of proceedings was at the top of the stairs where I sat with my skinny knees bumping nervously against my ears as if blocking out what I heard.

The Flying Squad would have won the fancy dress competition in the police force. They wore knee-length black leather boots with side buckles, tight navy blue/black trousers tucked into the boots and leather jackets and hats like motorcycle cops. I guess it made them go faster. The top cop barked for everyone to stay exactly where they were. Dad tried to ask the top cop to step into somewhere private but he wasn't having much to do with that. Meanwhile, people seemed to be giving names to eager scribbling cops that I'm sure I'd heard only on radio or on film. Names like Bob Menzies, Bing Crosby, Bob Hope. Waterstreets patrons didn't have the gift of disguise or the gab that a publican would wish. When a name was taken down the back door would open and the guests were allowed to leave one at a time. The sergeant commented on the good service in the dining room and wondered aloud how Dad made any money with such a large staff.

Suddenly Katherine Ann appeared like an angel behind me, breaking into Silent Night, Holy Night, All is calm, All is bright at the top of her voice. She had her First Communion dress on and was exercising her wonderful singing voice that had won the Chickabidee section of the Holdenson and Nielson radio show. Dad's dark brown eyes scaled the stairs a step at a time until they alighted upon Katherine Ann, who sensed her timing may not have been tickety boo so she turned on her black patent leather shoes and returned, singing more softly, to her bedroom. I think the sergeant thought the whole singing thing was a ruse.

I went to see if Mum was coming down. She stood in front of the make-up mirror in her best race day outfit holding a hairspray can in one hand and a bottle of perfume in the other. A couple of quick sprays into the air behind her back which she stepped carefully back into and then a spray into the air from the perfume in front of her which she waltzed through. She could be quick and thorough when she wanted. She could be strong too at times, despite the spells. She gave up sugar one Lent and never took it up ever again. She passed me quickly and negotiated the stairs gingerly towards Dad. The sergeant tipped his black leather cap. Mrs Street.

I do hope everything is all right, Sergeant. Bill's been rushed off his feet lately and I haven't been much help. Hope you'll forgive us. Drink?

She was very disarming for an unarmed mother. Before too long the cops were out the door and on their way and business was back to usual and the aprons piled into the corner for Monday's wash.

Sliding down the banisters until I banged my bum against the knob at the bottom, I dismounted and ran into the back bar. Mum was back in light work after a long spell and Dad poured her a shandy which she drank like mother's milk. There was never anything to worry about if she stuck to the shandies. Brandy and wine were her bellringers. The bottles of pink Porphyry Pearl at Christmas dinner literally flattened her. Dad loved the pineapple Porphyry but there was something in his chemistry that allowed him to take tons of it, except that he would burst into German songs like Ein Star Fell From Heaven One Beautiful Night. Different strokes. Mum's voice was like a squeaky wheelbarrow and I took after her in that department.

Four

September is the cruellest month when it's getting warmer and the baths hadn't yet opened so Dad suggested we drive out to the Weir for a swim. Mum flustered about telling everyone to get into their cossies and we packed a dozen Waterstreets Hotel imprinted terry towelling bath towels not yet pinched by boarders into the boot for Dad. He was so big that to lie by the Weir we had to open six of them together in a great square. When he laid on his stomach he was snoring in two seconds flat.

We put in a deflated tractor tube which we would blow up with the car pump, a pile of fruit at the bottom of the Esky with soft drink, beer bottles and ice over them to evade the Block, then some Moon Tiger coils to burn for the mossies which other bathers hated, the Sunday papers for re-reading, beer glasses, calamine lotion for when the sandflies bit, the new battery transistor which you had to hold in one hand facing north with one leg off the ground to work properly, Mum's big Black Hole wicker basket which she took everywhere, and a packet of Monte Carlo biscuits which we finished before we got out of the driveway. Dad leant his huge forearm out of the driver's window, slowing down at the Block, and in the straightest of straight voices, with a side wink and turn of the head, said No fruit; and was then ushered on by the khaki-shorted and shirty fruit fly inspector. Home free and Boathaven bound.

There's a place at the Weir called Boathaven where life's lottery winners who had houses on the sides of Forest Hills up under the Albury monument – like Hanrahan who owned the dry cleaners, Ferguson the bookmaker and Nesires the fashion house and haberdashers – kept their speedboats. We weren't ones for big toys, but Dad liked to go waterskiing if one of life's lottery winners invited him to go for a spin in one of their boats, usually called Lolita, Bikini, Hume Dambuster or, rarely, after the missus: Gwen, Edna or Agnes. With Dad's weight the boat needed a fair horsepower and sometimes when he fell off his water skies I'd run up and down the sides of the Weir yelling Tidal wave! and for everyone to move their towels up unless they wanted them to get wet.

Now with this Boathaven I didn't know if it was the chicken or the egg. When I first heard Beethoven, the muso's name, on 2CO, the ABC radio station, I thought it was the same as Boathaven, the speedboat parking spot of life's lottery winners. Or it could have been that I heard Ludwig's name first and thought that the luxury part of the Weir was named after him. Either way it led to some embarrassment later on when I claimed to have liked Boathaven's Fifth or that I thought the maestro lived at the Hume Weir.

All Mum and Dad did when they laid down the towel and blankets and cushions was fall straight to sleep. Katherine Ann, John, Peter and the Hood all climbed on board the huge tractor tyre and rode the rippled surf thrown up by the passing speedboats. We never seemed to judge our timetable by the clock at the Weir but by how red us kids' skins got. My back was some sort of sundial, used by my parents from the shade of the Holden to gauge the day. My blessed Bill, Mum would say, look how late it is. Charlie's red as a lobster. I think we'd better be off. Oh, we'll give him five minutes until he's nice and toasty.

I'd sit in mud on the bank and squelch it between my toes until it farted and Katherine Ann giggled, my back turning almost purple in the sun until it needed a safety pin to burst the blisters and a bottle of mercurochrome to kill infection.

The sun would be descending on the Victorian side of the Weir and you could see all the dead gums sticking out of the water from where they enlarged the Weir a couple of years before. They flooded the entire town of Tallangatta and everyone there was forced to sell up by Act of Parliament. The cemetery was even dug up so that there wouldn't be bodies of old Tallangattans floating down the river scaring people out of their wits. You couldn't see any of the old town which was far too deep, just all these dead trees and telegraph poles which made for fine fishing spots. Tallangatta had been moved lock, stock and barrel up the Kiewa Valley to somewhere new. They kept the name, but people said it never was the same town. The real Tallangatta died with the flooding.

I stared at those dead trees and imagined old dead and buried Tallangattans. The Atlantis of Albury and district was the lost city of Tallangatta and its widows who spent their entire lives tending gardens, the Royal Hotel, the town hall where many important issues in Tallangattan history were fought out, the corner store where credit was always available. Now all under water. And perhaps soon under fluoridated water, which might finally firm up the town's foundations. All of this started me thinking whether the fluoride in the Weir might affect the swimming, the speedboats or even the fishing. Imagine redfin with giant teeth. Dad may be right:

fooling with Nature is dangerous.

On the other hand, with fluoride you wouldn't have to clean your teeth all the time. Not that I did much, but I just forgot. They were yellowing at the bottoms. I was well into my second set. Your teeth will all fall out some day, cried Mum and Dad. With their dentured mouths they ought to talk. You can't have your caked teeth and eat with them too.

A lot of the speedboats had been sold off by life's lottery winners during Menzies Bloody Credit Squeeze and there were a lot of empty boatless buoys on the Weir. It had hit rich and poor alike but the rich felt it more I guess because they had more to lose. Aunt Faith said you can't miss what you don't have. She always spoke in those sorts of terms and when I said to her she used a lot of clichés, she just replied that a good cliché hits the nail on the head.

I don't know what it is about an expanse of water but it always gets me to thinking about things. It's something deep and spiritual. I see the Weir or the Mighty Murray, and usually next thing I'm sitting on my backside contemplating the infinite universe. The water has to be bigger than a bath, which doesn't do the trick, not even the Olympic pool. It has to be natural water. It's maybe because it's in my name. I'd probably faint if I ever saw the Specific Ocean, as Katherine Ann called it. A fortune teller at the Albury Show said I'm a

Cancer which is a water sign. It's everywhere I look.

This funny feeling mellows me out while my back slowly boils, while Dad snorts and starts in deep sleep with the transistor in his hand set on static, while Mum's asleep in the nest of leg at the back of Dad's knees with her mouth wide open, while the kids knock each other off the tyre and speedboats skim about the water like dragonflies and sound like Victa lawnmowers.

I know there are seven real wonders of the world. You won't find my wonders in the *Encyclopedia Britannica* that Dad bought off the travelling salesman last year. (The salesman said we got the set of encylopedias for free but we had to purchase a yearly subscription for updates. Dad said he'd have the set thank you and we'll write in the updates ourselves from someone else's.) Why are we here? Not at the Weir but on Earth? Why can't I stay up past ten at night? Why is Hayden Sir Sir Livermore so good at everything he does? I wonder why red-headed people always wear green, when Aunt Faith says red and green should never be seen. I wonder if truck drivers wear blue singlets to show off their tattoos, and are they born with them so they'll know straight away they are going to be truck drivers. I wonder if women really like sex – wouldn't it hurt? – or do they just like the idea of it. I wonder if the rubbing will make me go blind and I won't be able to see myself in Mum's three-dimensional swivelling make-up mirror. I wonder if there's life after death, or if it is the other way round. I wonder if I'll ever stop this eternal wondering, this wonderlust, and whether I'll ever settle down with a few good answers. I wonder why the Unchristian Brothers are always in a bad mood after they get a haircut. I wonder, will Brother Farrell be in a good mood first day back? He's always in a filthy one if he's had a haircut. The Unchristian Brothers cut each other's hair, and it's a rule of thumb that after the weekend hair-cutting sessions the Brothers are as cross as the southern sky. Their moods only get better as their hair grows back and then it's over and the cycle begins again. It's like their hair has feelings and needs novocaine when cut. Where did Dad really go when he said he was going to see a man about a dog? What is a wigwam for a goose's bridle that Mum and Dad always say when I ask some specific question like what did you get me for Christmas?

Anyway, the Weir's the biggest piece of water I've seen so far and it must be like holy water because I get watermelancholic when I watch it for too long. I get the wild blue wonder.

After a time Mum and Dad woke from the sleep of the dead to the world and we packed up the boot and washed our feet under the tap and got into the car for the trip home. We were always late for things, even surprise visits. It was ten miles between our pub and the Weir and about the same on the way back which was time for a dozen family songs, depending on how fast we went. Big Jeff Eames was supposed to open the back bar for the evening shift but he probably slept in or couldn't see the right key through the Band-aids and thumbprints on his bifocals.

Slow down, Bill, was Mum's constant chorus. She wouldn't let him pass loaded semi-trailers for fear their goods would tip over on to our car. If we could shut Katherine Ann up from singing Silent Night, Holy Night, All is calm, All is bright for a second some of the songs were real fun, especially if you knew the words, but if Dad didn't he'd make up his own which were better than the originals. Everyone loved the song about Sol Stein, the boarder in room 22. Dad called it *The Foggy Foggy Jew*.

When I was a publican I lived all alone
And I worked at the hotel trade
And the only only thing I did that was wrong
Was to woo the upstairs maid.

I wooed her in the winter time
Most of the summer too,
And the only only thing I did that was wrong
Was to keep it from the guy in 22.

One night she knelt down by my side
When I was fast asleep
She threw her arms around my neck
And then began to weep.

She wept, she cried, I bloody near died
Ah me, what could I do?
So all night long I held her in my arms
Unbeknownst to the guy in 22.

Again I am a publican, and I live with my son
We both work at the hotel trade
And every single time I look into his eyes
He reminds me of the upstairs maid.

He reminds me of the winter time
And of the summer too,
And of the many many times I held her in my arms
And I didn't tell the guy in 22.

Even Mum didn't mind that one, and sometimes late at night, with the bar lights out and only the green bulb over the till, she'd nudge someone to get Dad going with *The Foggy Foggy Jew*.

The car seemed to stop and start and jog as if in rhythm with the songs. A white (car slows) sports coat (slows again) and a pink (slows) carnation (faster)/I'm all dressed up (faster and faster) for the Prom. Then, if we were running late, If you knew

Susie like I know Susie; oh, oh, oh what a gal, and the next thing Malcolm Campbell's land and water speed record would be broken and the words couldn't even keep up as we were going faster than the speed of sound. Bill, Bill, slow down! with a foot stomp. We drove like bandits.

We loved it, sticking our heads out into the rushing air to dry or holding flicking towels trailing like streamers with the side windows wound up tight on them. But sometimes the towel would waft off on to the road and Dad would screech the Holden into a 180° turn and we'd go back and lean out and pick up the dirty towel.

Back at the pub it was into the shower, and the first realisation that your skin was bright red and Mum's Oil of Ulan brought only short relief which disappeared when the tropical short-sleeved shirt was almost surgically placed on me and buttoned up. It stuck like a gauze pad. Dad was glad to have Mum up and off to Aunt Faith's for dinner and cards. He had to open the bar for Big Jeff to serve and in next to no time we were at Aunt Faith's and only an hour or so late, which was earlier than the Faiths expected.

Aunt Faith served bottled beer to the parents with a plain brown bag still on the bottle to hide the label. Heavy opaque pewter cups with curvy handles were used to disguise the contents. Kids were served green cordial with water, never fizzy drinks, in Vegemite or Marmite jars. She said it was better for their teeth. When the fluoride comes we'll never have to clean them again and we'll be able to drink lemonade out of taps. It'll be Heaven on earth. Maybe Mum and Dad's teeth will grow back and they can throw away their dentures which float in glasses overnight by their bed, barely able to breathe, gasping for air.

Aunt and Uncle Faith were putting on a barbecue out the back in the pit they built with their own hands. It was lucky we were so late because Tom had to serve Benediction at St Joseph's in North Albury with Father Bongiorno and Aunt Faith always made everyone go. One thing you could say for Benediction is that it was shorter than Mass. It also had lots of incense and singing. Faith of Our Fathers, Holy Faith, We will be true to thee till death. We will be true to thee till death. On Sundays Benediction was an optional extra, like air conditioning, whereas Mass was compulsory.

Uncle Faith had this multi-pocketed apron with The World's Greatest Chef printed on it. He kept the chops and sausages turning over. Aunt Faith made a wonderful salad with her usual multitude of ingredients – tomato, lettuce, salt, pepper and Kraft dressing, in mysterious proportions. Kath, she said to her sister of me, he must have hollow legs. Eats like a horse. Look at him grow. Need to put a brick on his head. All this before I'd even taken a bite. It was nearly enough to put a boy off his food. But not quite.

After dinner Tom and I wanted to go for a swim in their above-ground 1000-gallon plastic pool but Aunt Faith said we couldn't go near water for two hours after eating. Not even under water from the sprinkler. Yes mein Führer, I whispered to Tom.

Growing up in the pub taught me all sorts of card tricks so I'd play my cousins stud poker or euchre instead of their usual fish and grab. Jimmy B had shown me how to keep a few aces up my shirtsleeves – even in summer with short sleeves. Cousins were easy beats and I yearned to play gin or poker with the grown-ups. Sometimes Dad would let me help him which was terrific. He played real cards for real money with the men from the Snowy River Hydroelectric Scheme on their week-end off.

Aunt Faith had cork coasters on the tasselled card blanket so there wouldn't be rings and every-one had their own ashtray imprinted with romantic views of Australia's great holiday resorts like the Blowhole at Kiama or the Three Sisters at Katoomba. She was a real neatnic. Dad complained about the flower vase in the middle of the table. You can't play cards properly if you're dealing around a bunch of bloody chrysanthemums. But

Aunt Faith was big on appearances and a picture of the Sacred Heart pointing to the hole in His ribcage after surgery looked kindly down on the card game. Jesus of the Sacred Heart had a real poker face. It was swell to be a real family again. Mum drinking shandies and even the occasional cup of tea and everyone saying how well she looked.

Tom and I went to his room where he showed off his faultless collection of plastic Spitfires, Mosquitoes, Messerschmitts, Zeros and Falcons that hung from the ceiling on strings or on plastic stands angled at take-off. Tom could have been a surgeon. Every piece of each plane was in its proper place. Not a smear of Tarzan's Grip on any of them. My efforts produced wings on tails, big gobs of glue solidifying over the cockpit and the plane in a nosedive, if it made the stand at all. I had too many ants in my pants for these toys, Aunt Faith believed. Still, I loved Tom's room where he was made to make his own bed every morning, had a bedside lamp instead of the torch I used, had a quilt made by his mum and his toys packed so neatly that you had to make a reservation to use them.

After a while I went back to the card table where Aunt Faith's eyes were rolling about the bottom of her glasses like brown mercury looking at Mum to see if the shandies were affecting her.

Whenever they were talking about adult stuff Aunt Faith would nod towards me and say the walls have ears. At first I'd look behind me to check and there was only the formation of ceramic ducks that Taillight would have loved to have a shot at. Then I got it.

Aunt Faith's hair was a sort of khaki when I was just a kid and suddenly turned blue overnight like Aunt Charity's who lived in Macauley Street around the corner from the pub. If it was something in the water that turned women's hair blue when they turned thirty, perhaps the fluoride might fix it. Aunt Charity used to tip me to go to the chemist's for her dye. She didn't want anyone to know her blue hair wasn't natural.

Mum was holding her own and her cards as well and Dad and she had huge piles of matches in front of them. One thing about pub life: you had to be able to play cards or you were dead. The North Albury suburbanites couldn't cut it with a pair of publicans even if their son was a plastic aeronautical engineer.

Back home Mum kissed me a beery goodnight and tried to find my school uniform in the pile that had passed for laundry since school had broken up. She pulled some of the creases out of the pants and shirt and laid them carefully out between layers of newspaper and told me to lift the mattress so I could sleep on them. They'll be brand spanking new in the morning. Good night and God bless. Say your prayers.

I got out the torch and read World War Two in Pictures under the blanket until I fell asleep in a wet flannel wonderworld.

Five potato

Barton, Glen?
    Present.
Present what?
Present Sir.
Bahrij, Robert?
Present Sir.
Carrick, Richard?
Present Sir.
Capile, Gerry?
Present Sir.
Clarkson, Robert?
Present Sir.
Collins, Michael?
Present Sir.
Skip a few.
Toth, Tibor?

Present Sir.

Skip a few more.

Vaughan, Stephen?

Present Sir.

Brother Farrell's roll call of the survivors of the third term of First Year Gold at St Thomas Aquinas in North Albury revealed a few absentees and one drop-out. Terry Freyer of the fighting Freyers of South Albury, who took on the little Thursday Islander on the big drum in the last Jimmy Sharman's Travelling Boxing Show and won, had joined his father's business of being unemployed full-time. It would only be a matter of time before he graduated to unemployable and had a brood of young fighting Freyers himself and got Social Security cheques in his own name. He would be missed. He was a great farter and could do it at will, clearing the classroom if Brother Farrell's questions got too tricky.

Waterstreet, Charles?

Absent Sir.

A perfectly aimed finger of white chalk rifled towards my head out of Brother Farrell's hand at the speed of light, bouncing off my forehead like an untipped arrow. There'll be no skylarking this term young Mr Waterstreet. Get yourself up the front. Luckily it was still cold in the classroom despite the near heatwave outside and I had on a jumper whose sleeves I pulled down over my knuckles and held in place through motholes with my white thumbs. Six of the best for you young man. Not a bad start to the last term. Didn't even get through the first roll call.

Yensch, John?

Present Sir.

I just couldn't help myself. It's the waiting that kills you. Words escaped from my mouth before I knew they were even there. My tongue was cheese inside a mousetrap. Left hand first thank you young man. If you kept the crook of your arm slightly bent and thumbs through the holes you could leave the edge of your jumper over your wrist and lower palm which otherwise would really sting if the strap hit you there. It's time for a little of the John Thomas. That's what Brother Farrell called his 15 inch by one inch thick leather strap stitched by my very own uncle, Bob Carrol the bootmaker. He made straps for all the Albury Unchristian Brothers. Brother Farrell kept his deep inside one of the long slits of side pockets in his ruffled black habit. Three whacks on each hand. The trick was not to cry or show any pain which required a lot of pre-hand warming like sitting on your hands if you felt the strap a-coming or rubbing your hands together on the way up the aisle. My bloody mouth got me in more trouble than the whole rest of me.

The walk back was as bad as the walk up. A stay of execution from the Governor does not assist the condemned man who has to walk from the scaffold back down the stairs and back to his cell to wait for the next deadline. The fear of the strap faced every boy every day. At least the strap did hit the right spot on both wrists of the pullover. The stinging only lasted forever.

St Thomas Aquinas' school uniform was a curious mixture of the practical and ideological. Summer uniform was a set of khaki cotton shorts and short sleeved shirt with a green and yellow striped tie. We looked like little Diggers. Albury in winter can get so cold that it snowed once at night and Mum woke up and thought the A-bomb had dropped. Puddles froze over in panes of ice. The winter uniform was woollen shorts and short sleeved cotton shirt with a grey jumper and coat. It got so cold Brother Farrell would have to kick the back of your knees to make you bend your legs to kneel at church. A set of blue and red mercurochromed grazed knees seemed to be part of the school uniform. The school cap was a green woollen small-peaked grease trap for Brylcreem with the school motto yellow-stitched on in tiny Latin that not even Hayden Sir Sir Livermore could translate. You could keep a car running on a single cap for a year, Dad said.

Ever since I was a kid, I think my whole personality and attitude to life has been forged by having a surname beginning with one of the last letters of the alphabet. Unless there was a Xavier or a Yensch or a Zerbst in the class, I was nearly always the last one to do everything. Sometimes that was peachy, like cleaning the blackboard dusters, but generally it led to me being late for everything because I'm always the one called upon last. In my next life I'm coming back as Arthur Aardvark. Another thing it made me was a great procrastinator which I'll get around to telling you about one day.

After roll call and corporal punishment, it was the Headmaster's welcome over the loudspeaker. This wonderful device was fitted in each classroom and avoided the need for too many quadrangle assemblies which could lead to school riots and mass giggling. Brother Mazorinie from the safety of his office tapped the mike three times and tested one, two, three followed by shortwave noises. Everything started with prayers and finished with prayers. Even prayers had prayers in the middle of them. Every period had prayers and Religious Knowledge for God's sake had prayers. Brother Mazorinie sang Hail Queen of Heaven the Ocean Star, Guide of the Wanderer Here Below and we all sang along as loudly as we could from our desks, competing with the microphone and loudspeakers. At school, before the invention of electricity and loudspeakers, the push button megaphone held sway at general assembly.

Big things were expected this term with the fifth year doing final examinations for the Leaving Certificate. The loudspeaker warned:

> Do not, repeat *do not* put JMJ [Jesus Mary and Joseph] or AMDG [Latin for good luck or something] on top of any public exam papers. Some markers hold it against the Catholics. They look for any excuse to mark down the Catholics.

I would have thought that St Thomas Aquinas School on the front cover and names like O'Brien, O'Halloran, Murphy and Purtle might give the game away. Francis Xavier O'Connell had better change his name by deed poll if he wanted to pass.

Football season was now over and the Head-master expected us to knuckle down to the job in hand which caused a cackle of laughter at the back of each class. Ahead of us was the feast day of All Saints and All Souls which brought a smile to everyone's face because it meant an extra holiday. It's little wonder Catholics were downtrodden, we had so many feast days off school we could never catch up with public boys. There was to be an inter-school Athletic Carnival which didn't interest me unless it was against St Mary's Girls School where I might stand a chance. I ran like a startled giraffe.

Finally, with a tinge of the Irish accent he never quite lost despite fifty years of his fifty-five having been spent in Australia, the Headmaster announced there was the matter of the fluoride. The Brothers in charge of each class will be telling you more about this later, but His Holiness Pope John XXIII himself has turned his mind to the question and although it is not an article of faith, like meat on Friday, he will be making a statement in the very near future. In the mean time, just think of this: would you like to have been baptised with fluoridated holy water? Just ask yourself that question. Good day and God bless you. Now everyone stand and sing Faith of our Fathers, Holy Faith, We will be true to thee till death. We will be true to thee till death.

Brother Farrell's first period of the day for First Year Gold was Geometry. First year and beyond was broken into two groups. The brainy types went into Gold and the apparently less brainy into Black. It sort of set the scene for self-esteem. First Year Black were the boys who ended up with eagle tattoos on their forearms, who wore suits after leaving school only for funerals and court appearances, and who married large girls in clogs who seemed to fall pregnant the first time they went to the drive-in. In First Year Gold we studied Latin which was a very handy subject, being a language unspoken in society for over a thousand years. I mean if ever you found yourself in a time machine going backwards, it would be an indispensable tool. Latin prepared you for the priesthood, medicine or pharmacy, occupations unlikely to attract anyone in First Year Black who, on the other hand, studied a subject of doubtful utility called Geography. Not much help if you were never going to leave Albury anyway. Still, they learnt that Albury was 734 feet above sea level which made you dizzy just thinking of it.

In Gold we got a bit of the informal Geography, mostly maps of Australia and Asia chalked on one of the blackboards earlier in the year in Religious Knowledge and never erased. From Asia, in particular China, there was a huge yellow arrow arching down with its tip touching the pointy end of Queensland and covering most of south-east Asia including the area formerly known as Ceylon. This image haunted me every night of every day of that year. It was the spread of Communism carrying in its wake the vicious hatred of Catholics and their families.

In primary school, Unchristian Brother after Unchristian Brother chalked the board with the same message map and my nightmares involved Chinese hordes swarming up Smollett Street from the railway station, slaughtering mums and dads and children. They'd travel by rail, probably without tickets. The Weir was sure to be a prime target for their bombs, now bloated with water stretched over old Tallangatta. There were six hundred million of them when I was seven. Well, now there's a billion and they're going at it like myxo-immune rabbits. They're still not here but I curled up in bed at night with a wooden ruler under my pillow in case of attack. No wonder I wet the bed.

You might think Communism had nothing to do with schooling but you'd be wrong. It was a subject in itself. The mummy's boys would have a geometry set in a zippered-up bag with their names in thick black ink on the side. It contained a compass with a sharp point and a pencil for the drawing of circles, a set square which was strangely a plastic triangle, a protractor which sounds gynaecological but was a plastic semicircle, and a set of divides with two pointy ends which was for measuring distances and poking the boy in front of you in the bum. Not being a mummy's boy, I had one of Jimmy B's nails tied to a piece of string which was then tied to a pencil at the other end. This was for the drawing of the circle. You didn't get much of a difference in the radius but you got consistency. I had a ruler in inches and centimetres and a rubber for mistakes of which there were many. There was much borrowing of other boys' instruments for Geometry.

My other projects suffered from the leaking of fountain pens which seemed to run or blot whenever I touched them. Biros were frowned upon as the sort of things only heathens or conmen would use.

Using a blackboard duster as a pointer Brother Farrell traced the familiar yellow route south from China to Albury, noting with a flourish where Russia was, and that already it was too late to save most of Europe. Holy pictures of the saints looked on from the walls nodding in agreement. We sat in our chairs with our mouths open like the laughing clowns at the Show, heads turning from side to side following Brother Farrell across the floor. It's a wonder no one put a ping pong ball in our mouths.

Then came the message. These Communists were cunning, powerful and baffling. One of their devious plots to take over Australia and eventually Albury was to weaken the desire in the menfolk to fight. The less desire, the easier it would be for them to defeat us. I didn't have much of the desire, but I had the fear and the trembles. The plan they had engineered with their tricky oriental minds was to put this stuff in the water which would take away the will to shoot back, to fight hand-to-hand, and to take a stand. This stuff was fluoride. Brother Farrell spelt it in yellow chalk. Take this message home with you and tell your parents. We can take no chances in the fight against Communism. Tell them to vote against the fluoride in the referendum.

Then he drew a few circles and squares and that was Geometry for the day. There was an Our

Father who art in Heaven, Hallowed be thy name
to end Geometry and one to begin Social Studies
with Brother Kelvin. Brother Kelvin was from the
Queensland Irish which meant he had a fiery temper to match his wispy orange hair and small brown
darty eyes. The visible parts of his body were
covered in sunspots and only the Unchristian
Brothers who showered with him or perhaps
Brother Tesario knew if the sunspots only gloved
his hands and pockmarked his head. Brother Tesario was the teacher who disappeared to another
smaller country town one day after an incident, as
Brother Mazorinie described it over the loudspeaker, with the vaulting horse. He would forever
be standing next to the horse with a helping hand
under the boys' buttocks and beyond if the bounce
from the trampoline didn't quite get them across the
length of the horse. After the incident he had been
transferred to non-teaching duties in the outback.
We worried for the sheep.

Brother Kelvin himself would flare like a sun-
spot over the smallest thing, so if we mucked up we
tried to keep it as small as possible. His trip-wire
temper so permeated Social Studies that you could
hear a boy frown, such was the tense silence. You
could hear a pin if not the penny drop. I had a kind
of photogenic memory (you should see my brain
scans) but didn't dare answer anything for fear a
wrong one would incur an outbreak of straps or

backhanders. Greg Esler was sent home last term for saying wheelbarrow in front of class. Esler caught his shin on the iron leg of his desk and cried out wheelbarrow. Brother Kelvin turned on a six-pence from the blackboard like he had eyes in the back of his head which he may well have and there wouldn't be much hair in front of them either. Why did you say wheelbarrow, Esler? Because me mum says wheelbarrow whenever she drops something or something goes wrong. Why wheelbarrow, Esler? She says it's better to say that than fuck. He didn't even have time to clear out his desk before going to the outpatients at the Sisters Without Mercy Hospital.

Brother Kelvin's body movements were like those in old silent pictures. When he cleaned the blackboard he almost disappeared in a snowstorm of chalk. He'll probably die of calcium asphyxia. Waterstreet, what's the capital of Chile? C, Sir. I've got the worst case of verbal diarrhoea. Just can't help myself. A born smart alec. Luckily he didn't hear it or everyone's hand-held guffawing, and I then said Santiago Sir, too loudly.

The early term project was to be on the fluori-dation of the water supply, pro and con, which my Latin helped me know was for and against. Brother Kelvin made it pretty clear that the party line should be maintained against it but insisted that the project should be as always on large pieces of pink or blue cardboard, sold at newsagents, with pictures cut out of magazines and writing in coloured Derwent pencils. He suggested photos of teeth before and after the Communists poured bags marked with skulls and crossbones into the Weir at night, a boy sitting in a dentist's chair, the history of teeth through the ages like from baby to adult and/or from prehistoric times before Cleaver Bunton was mayor to modern times. His help left little for our imaginations to do. It had to be in in a fortnight or there'd be Hell to pay. I had thought Hell was a word like wheelbarrow but obviously not from Brother Kelvin's lips.

The pealing of the bells from the Sacred Heart Church indicated midday and time for the Angelus, then it was Religious Knowledge and finally lunch. The bells of St Pat's in downtown Albury were real bells with thick ropes from a real limestone tower in St Pat's Church. The Sacred Heart used a huge loudspeaker and a 78 rpm record of bells pealing. Sometimes the needle jumped. It just wasn't the same. It didn't ring true. You could only hear the record for a couple of blocks. It was barely audible at the football end of the school building. If peace broke out most of North Albury wouldn't know.

I skipped morning teatime which was really morning without teatime because all we got was free milk which was a million years old with a couple of inches of thick yellow cream at the top.

The ¼-pint bottles had been sitting in crates in the sun for hours just to get the right pukey temperature to make you vomit. I think the government has been slipping fluoride into the milk for years on the side. You couldn't bite a hole in the silver milk bottle tops because they would zing your fillings like an electric shock. You could peel them off with a bitten fingernail which was hard because most were bitten down to the second knuckle, or you could stick a well-aimed first finger into it.

Religious Knowledge meant memorising the Green Catechism. Who made the world? God made the world. Who is God? God is the creator of all things finite and infinite. Then there'd be the lives of the saints, or near saints. Some were great like Father Damien of the South Pacific whose longevity is now assured in my family. Leper stories made us laugh our heads off but deep down we were enthralled. St Lawrence the patron saint of cooks who was being roasted over coals by infidels asked to be turned over as that side was done.

Brother Farrell took this class and sometimes the Big Questions would be posed. Would you go to Hell if you lived a blameless life for fifty years, going to confession every week, then once had an impure thought and entertained it and were run over by a bus before you got to confession? The correct answer was yes, you would go to Hell. What of God's love? Rules are rules. God in His infinite mercy was cruel but fair. On the other hand, you could commit sin all your life, be going down in an aeroplane, say an Act of Perfect Contrition and crash and die and go straight to Heaven. An Act of Perfect Contrition was never far from my lips when Dad was driving.

My personal favourite saint was Augustine who committed every type of sin imaginable before converting and living the life of a perfect Catholic. Augustine would be my role model if I could only get the timing right for the quick conversion. As late as possible and after committing every type of sin imaginable. Not just breaking the Ten Commandments but variations on those themes. Not just the rubbing but the rubbing with others. Maybe even incest, bestiality, buggery, torture, stealing over ten pounds, hijacking covered wagons, inflicting crucifixions, laughing in church, peeing in the baptismal font. The list was inexhaustible. No matter what, Augustine had done it. The mind boggled. He had the right idea. I would appropriate the Augustine Attitude. Like if you had a dirty thought, entertained it, then that was a mortal sin. Off to Hell in a basket if a bus hit you. You may as well do the bloody thing as think about it.

The trouble was, in First Year Gold there were no girls to do it with and I wouldn't know what to do anyway. Then I'll do it with the tartan cushion and not just dream about it all day. There were no degrees of mortal sin. It was just like Brother Farrell drew on the blackboard: a state of grace was a round chalk circle with nothing in it. Venial sins were specks and spots inside the circle. Mortal sin was where you laid the finger of chalk on its side and coloured the whole circle white. A mortal could be thinking of doing it or just plain doing it. You may as well do it. That was the Augustine Attitude. That was for me.

Brother Farrell told us the story of creation. First day God made the light. Second day He made the waters and sky. The third day the Earth and plants. The fourth day He made the sun, moon and stars. The fifth day He made birds. The sixth day He made animals. Finally, He rested on the seventh day. Any questions? Sir, Sir. My hand darted up and down as if pulling on a toilet chain to ask a question. Yes, Waterstreet. If God only made the sun on the fourth day, how did He measure the first three days? Clever little dick. By His watch. Next.

Religious Knowledge left more questions unanswered than all of Augustine's sins put together. It was an endless cycle, interrupted mercifully by the lunch bell over the loudspeaker and prayers before dispersing into the playground for mutton sandwiches lovingly prepared by Mrs Westie and lime cordial in a plastic thermos if I'd remembered. I was proud to say fruit never touched my lips if I had any say. Vegetables were for the birds and grownups.

Lunch was eaten on tables and strong wooden stools cemented into the ground around tall red gum trees that were allowed to grow for shade. Of course the shade at lunchtime was on the other side of the trees where no tables and stools were cemented into the ground. Boys actually lost weight during lunch with all the heat and sweating. The New Australian boys brought exotic foods in silver foil packed into plastic Tupperware. The stuck-up ones had their sandwiches cut into little triangles for easy eating. Mrs Westie didn't bother cutting the mutton sandwiches. You'd need a chainsaw anyway.

In the playground my palate was introduced to such exquisite tastes as camp pie, salami, Peck's anchovy paste, baloney sausage by the Abacair boy, cheese wrapped in plastic individual slices without silver paper, cheese with holes, coloured cheese would you believe from the migrant kids, triple decker sandwiches, hot peppers, two types of chicken, dark and white, Vegemite with or without jam. Mums would turn in their graves at home if they knew that their sons were swapping their loving healthy sandwiches for who-knows-what with kids who wore leather-aproned shorts to school.

No one ever wanted Mrs Westie's mutton, although it had been kept fresh in the meat cabinet for months. Neither did I after I couldn't get a piece of thick string out of my back teeth one afternoon. When I complained she said it was for flossing behind the big teeth. Mrs Westie either overdid the cooking in which case it was black and as thick as Bob Carrol's leather uppers or underdid it so you could still read the blue writing on the skin of the mutton. I think it must have been the sheep's name. They died of old age. And this was before date stamping was introduced. Her mutton would have been lucky to be dated this century.

After this repast, marbles were the order of the day although the acres of cement made it hard to keep the marbles from rolling all over the place. I had a favourite Steelo made of stainless steel which I flicked like a mighty bullet with my thumb. In my exuberance I once flicked it down my gullet and ran home where Mum got Dr Twomey on the phone who told her that like all things it would soon pass. I watched my turds like a hawk for a week but it slipped away under cover of darkness somehow. Mrs Westie wouldn't let me use the vegetable strainer. It may still be in me, resting, waiting ready to pop out with a plonk when I'm having a lazy crap. I've always got one ear cocked for the sound, no matter how much time goes by.

Some mummy's boys had home-made marble bags with pull-through string. God made school uniforms with lots of pockets for marbles. You shouldn't interfere with His plans. Unless of course you got a hole in the pocket and your finger could reach your willie while you were walking or sitting in class. I don't think God had that in mind.

Brother Kelvin's English class was always after lunch, more prayers and toilet. You're not allowed to go ones or twos between the end of lunch and break-up. Once Stephen Vaughan put his hand up to go during Litany but Brother Kelvin shook his head. Vaughan weed himself at about Holy of Holies, Pray for us and blushed redder than Brother Kelvin himself.

The Bible for English was *Poems of Spirit and Action*. Dad had mighty midnight poetry classes of the pub kind, when he'd call for silence with his huge hands outstretched, padding the air in front of him, and the rhubarb sound would still and he'd begin with all the Jacks sitting upright on their barstools:

Into the valley of Death
Rode the six hundred.
Cannon to right of them
Cannon to left of them.

That wasn't in *Poems of Spirit and Action*; it should have been. We had a favourite one in the book about Australia called *My Country* by Dorothea Mackellar. She was the sort of Queen Mother of Australian poetry. In our school book the pages weren't very wide so that if a word didn't fit at the end of a line it would be half finished, hyphenated and finished off on the next line. Such was our *My Country*, which unfortunately for the poet but to our huge glee we recited like this:

I love a sunburnt count-
ry,
A land of sweeping plains

Boy, did we accent that last syllable of the first line. To this day Brother Kelvin has no idea why we always asked if we could recite it. He thought we were patriotic and poetic, not the pathetic dirty little boys we were.

English was Greek to most of the boys in First Year Black. The way English was taught sort of took the fun out of reading. There were more laughs on the toilet doors than in most essays we studied and most of the kids in First Year Black thought Shakespeare was a pub in Ballarat.

Brother Taylor took us for the last two periods of Science and Maths interrupted only by the three o'clock Litany. Science was the combination of the unknowable in the form of Physics with the unteachable in the form of Chemistry. The only difference most could see between the two was their spelling. Test tubes, Bunsen burners, pipettes, prisms were all toys for the nerds. Maths involved the use of the slide rule, which was an elevated form of finger counting.

The only break from the learning was the Litany. Brother Taylor lead off with Mother of Grace and we'd all say Pray for us and then Holy of Holies, Pray for us; Hope of the hopeless, Pray for us; Tabernacle of the Most High, Pray for us; and this went on for ten minutes or so. Sometimes we'd say Grace Brothers, a Sydney department store, instead of Pray for us, and Brother Taylor would stop mid-prayer and we'd mumble Grace Broth . . . and go all red. Not as red as him though and he'd clip the nearest boy over the back of the head and start all over again.

If you weren't on detention you'd catch Martin's bus out the front and if you were quick you'd get the seat facing the driver whose wide steering wheel made him look like an exotic sea captain except for his grey shorts and long white socks. The closing doors sounded like giant farts and everyone would giggle and wave a hand in front of their faces much to the distaste of the captain in shorts who eyed the rear vision mirror with a weatherbeaten frown.

My Globite school case sat clutched between my thin legs like a bride on the night before her wedding. The captain in shorts hit every pothole between Lavington and Wodonga sending bags and boys into the air like young crash test dummies, bouncing around as if on a trampoline with coins and marbles coming out of our pockets and running every which way down the aisle. The bus eventually pulled up in front of the pub and released me with a hiss.

Six potato

A t the back window near the side gate to the laneway I'd reach for a packet of Smith's potato chips when Dad wasn't looking and shove it up the back of my jumper and then ask for a squash. Dad said that there was some wine needing bottling out the back. But I've got my homework to do. Homework, homework, I'll give you bloody homework. He threw me the hotel keys, a huge jailer's bunch of keys of all types for every room in the pub plus some. The wine room was an old bedroom which contained old wooden beer boxes lined up along three walls, stacked on top of each other to the roof. The boxes contained all three types of wine known to man: white, tawny and brown, whose initials were written in ink on fresh corks and plonked into handwashed returned beer bottles. Three large wooden kegs of white, tawny and brown sat on their sides on top of other kegs with huge cork stoppers. The bottling of wine, a task that fell to the firstborn and would be passed in turn on to the boy children down to the Hood when I went to boarding school, involved more physics than Brother Farrell ever dreamed of.

After uncorking the vat, with a fork from Mrs Westie's drawers if necessary, a rubber tube was dangled through the hole into the wine. Care must be taken to avoid exposing the wine to too much air as the dreaded wine fly would lay eggs on the surface and buzz about pissed as a fart and although it was still drinkable if you delicately scooped the eggs off the surface with a spoon and didn't tell anyone, the edge was off the wine, especially as it was unusually fresh having just been made and gumboot-crushed by Barney Gehrig down in Barnawatha where Taillight and I swam in his large vats of wine while rabbit shooting, but that's another story.

At my First Communion I swore to the Bishop of Wagga Wagga that liquor would not pass my lips until I was 25. He unilaterally bumped up the usual age from 21 in a holy fit of unfairness. However, the bottling required me to suck the wine through the rubber hose, while my mouth was lower than the other end of the hose inside the keg, until the wine gushed up the hose, then just before it hit the end,

I'd clamp my finger over the hose-hole and shove it into the upright empty beer bottle until the wine reached just above the Carlton & United arrow, when I'd clamp the hose again and try to shove it to the next bottle and so on. Not once did the wine, be it white, tawny or brown, ever not run into my cheek-sucked face. At first I had an almighty guilt that I'd let down the Bishop of Wagga Wagga, but later I reasoned that if liquor had passed my lips I may as well be hung for a sheep as a lamb and I sucked that sucker until I was singing Danny Boy, the pipes, the pipes are calling, From glen to glen and down the mountainside, till the cows came home to roost.

Not all Mum's and Dad's after school jobs and messages led to hangovers but the bottling was a tradition I took to like a duck to water. In the highest boxes near the ceiling Dad had the long bottles of Porphyry Pearl Banana and Pineapple that we'd break out at Christmas, feast days and on holy days of obligation. The ends of their necks stuck out like boarders too big for their beds. A single pearl light bulb hung on a cord from the ceiling. I could fill a dozen bottles in less than 100 seconds on a good day.

Dad sold this special wine in beer bottles at a significant discount on the labelled stuff. Many a drunk depended on it to fit a seven-days-a-week drunk into his pension cheque. It was tight but with some belt-tightening they could manage. You'd have to bring an empty beer bottle to exchange for a full one. The beer companies hated it and took legal remedies to stop it. So Dad wrapped newspaper around the bottle and stuck sticky tape around the neck so no one could see what you were drinking. Someone would present an empty beer bottle at the bar, ask for a bottle of white, tawny or brown and get a neatly newspaper-wrapped bottle with a white, tawny or brown initial inked on to the cork and then it was off to their lonely room to drink it out of the bottle or a chipped enamel tea mug or cracked Vegemite jar. We made money and everyone was happy, especially me after an hour of the bottling. Dad called it part and parcel of the great business re-cycle after Menzies Bloody Credit Squeeze.

The pipes the pipes were calling me for dinner, and afterwards Mum was taking everyone to see a film on fluoride that had been made in Tasmania. She and Dad had not made up their minds – or rather, as Dad put it, she had not made up their minds – on the fluoride question. I've an open mind, Mum said. Although Dad had a downstairs bar view, he hadn't told Mum. The rest of the town was in a fury one way but mostly the other.

The weather was getting warmer but it was still ideal for Mum to take the foxhead stole with tail out of the clothes closet to wear to the Civic Theatre for the Fluoride Forum. Dignitaries from as far afield as Queensland had taken the Spirit of Progress train to Albury or the Daylight Express from Melbourne to speak at the Great Debate. Monday night was Commercial Club night for Dad, where he played competition snooker and cards and ate fish and chips late at Font's Fish Café, where Voula flirted with her customers, much to Con's disgust. But tonight there would be no snooker, his screw-in cue stick with its own metal container and handle would stay at home upright in the corner of the clothes closet.

Mum, although slightly tipsy from a couple of shandies, kept steady on her stilettos and was made up like a Mates mannequin when she went out. Katherine Ann had her First Communion dress on, John and Peter were in school uniforms and the Hood was in the pram even though he'd been walking for a couple of years. Dad touched his side pockets for his Viscounts like a gunslinger, the packet he was using and a spare. Mum had hers in the Blue-Black Hole leather purse in which the entire fortune in money and goods of her side of the family was contained. It was a bottomless pit. Her hand entered and excited it like a magician pulling endless scarves from a sleeve. A woman's purse is best left unexplored by young boys.

Smoking I think was compulsory during the Great Debate on Fluoride in the public hall at the

Civic Theatre. Redhead matches constantly exploded in small sparks of life in the semi-dark, everyone puffed away, blue smoke streaming down from the ceiling and along the walls as in a battle-field, while the speakers debated whether fluoride would affect the good health of Albury's citizens and their children and their children's children. If Albury had had a television station like Shepparton the event couldn't have been televised except with an infra-red camera and a massive spotlight.

The mayor had cast his not inconsiderable weight and dignity, but not his office, behind the Anti-Fluoridation Committee headed by Alderman Roach and his wife. The Fluoridation Committee was an amalgam of Albury dentists. The first speaker suggested that fluoridation was a dental plot, that fluoridation might lead to teeth staying in the children's heads longer and that that would lead to more cavities and thus more work for dentists. The current situation meant teeth fell out early and dental plates which lasted for life were inserted and the dentists were deprived of money. It's hard to grapple with this logic. The Anti-Fluoridation Com-mittee speakers were at the cutting edge.

There were three speakers from each side and then questions from the floor after the film. There was trouble with the projector but someone from the Regent was on hand to lend one. Mayor Bunton adjudicated fairly straight down the middle of the

Anti-Fluoridation case. The Hood pushed his pram up and down the aisle of the Civic Theatre with Peter and John inside. Katherine Ann hummed *Silent Night* and dreamed of the time she'd sing again at the Albury Eisteddfod in this very same auditorium before much the same crowd against girls from all over the Riverina with their bathroom-best voices, singing their soon-to-bloom breasts out.

Hacking coughing punctuated the evening like giant frogs with the 'flu. I coughed a little just to keep up. It could have been passive smoke inhalation. Aunts Faith, Hope and Charity were all there. Aunt Faith must have had a tipple because she genuflected on one knee towards the stage before taking her seat. Force of a lifetime's habit. Aunt Charity was unmarried but kept company with a man who had a gigantic red setter dog, which waited with its long red tongue out on the front porch of Aunt Charity's on Friday nights while his master slept inside Aunt Charity's powder blue bedroom with four polystyrene wig stands with four wigs in shades of blue. A platoon of perfume bottles stood shoulder to shoulder on her dressing table and thick white shag-pile carpet crept halfway up the walls. It got sticky in there during the long wet season.

The Unchristian Brothers and the Sisters Without Mercy from St Joseph's had sent small but interested contingents. People from all walks of what passes for life in Albury were in the Civic Theatre.

In fact two films were shown. Both were pro-fluoridation. An Anti-Fluoridation Committee speaker suggested they had been backed by the world-wide aluminium combine, as fluoride is a by-product of aluminium. If every small town and city in Australia used 20 lbs of it a day, this would make quite a fortune for the combine. Heads nodded either in agreement or shook in disagreement, depending on points of view. The undecided nodded their heads diagonally.

The Tasmanian film *One in a Million* traced the history of children's teeth in the small township of Beaconsfield over seven years of fluoridation and its testing. It certainly needed a Peter Finch or an Audie Murphy to liven it up a bit. It was in black and white and claimed success for fluoride but who would want to live in Tasmania, I thought. Too high a price for a good set of teeth. The surprise packet was the colour second feature film from America, *Drop in a Bucket*. Decay was cut by two-thirds in the US town of Hillerdale. Everyone in it spoke like Kirk Douglas. The Anti-Fluoridation Committee produced no films, no pictures, no charts, just well-balanced arguments said Mayor Bunton. You couldn't pull the wool over Albury's eyes with gimmicks.

Mum had this bee in her bonnet about the fluoride. She couldn't decide one way or the other but was hungry for information. Unfortunately she was a little thirsty for it too and during a break Mum and Dad slipped all of us over to the Albion Hotel for squashes and a shandy for herself. Aunt Hope, not a drinker herself although she had been a barmaid at Nana's pubs since she could crawl, joined us in the beer garden with Nana herself. Nana Waterstreet had been racked with the pain of standing and serving behind bars all her life and had yards of brown bandages wrapped like a mummy underneath her stockings. You could see the mound of safety pins that kept them in place. She complained about the ache of what sounded like asparagus veins.

Katherine Ann wandered off and we lost her for half an hour of the intermission. We went to the police station to report it and she was there in front of the counter leading the constables in a chorus of *Silent Night*. We were late returning to the second half of the Great Debate.

Equal time had been allocated to the Yes and No lobbies. The No group had imported Mr J.E. Harding from Rockhampton in Queensland who singlehandedly turned the fluoride tide in Chinchilla, Biloela, Tenterfield, Tully and Orange. He had a fine speaking voice and such charm people would have put arsenic in the water if he asked them to. Some suggested he was a proponent of government-supplied apples, medium to small, to Queensland school children. Apples were good. Fluoridation was bad.

The Yes men were led by Rotarian Stuart Macdonald and our family dentist Len Stern. Another leading Rotarian, Mr Chick, supported it. The films had swayed these Rotarian minds, and Mr Harding found folded papers in his top pocket that revealed mice having bladder stones in tests involving fluoridation in 645 mice. Further, other documents from his trouser pocket indicated there was evidence of Mongolism where fluoridated water was drunk. Dad looked at Mum worriedly when he boomed about the malfunctioning of the thyroid glands. Dad's side of the family had been plagued with thyroid problems since photography at least had been invented. Family photographs of Waterstreets showed great-grandmothers with Father Christmas chins going down their chests in bibs of flesh. Dad himself was growing jowls at the same rate as Mario Lanza. We didn't know if it was the thyroid or Mrs Westie's food. Dad didn't need any help from the fluoride.

The Yes men were mostly dentists and doctors. They all started their addresses with Unaccustomed as I am to public speaking . . . The No men had the gift of the gab. It was a lay down misere. Mayor Cleaver Bunton spoke of personal freedom and of the Christian belief to decide what should be done with our bodies. He claimed that there was no real evidence of a Communist plot to sap our vitality but added that the recent A-bomb tests were putting Strontium 90 into the atmosphere and in the body it joined with fluoridated water to expose the body to increased internal radiation. But the real reason to vote No was that we should not experiment on Albury families. Australia's first inhabitants ate only what was found on the plains, in the rivers or streams, and had mouthfuls of gleaming white teeth. Black Bungambrewatahians were always drawn and painted smiling, even as the white men stole their lands from underneath their wide noses and grins. On whose shoulders lies the fault of tooth decay? [White parents' sugary hands, I should think.] Furthermore, could it be supposed that a wise Creator, foreseeing the future of all mankind, would not dispense what is just right in the composition of every raindrop? Can the Creator have neglected to add a teeny weeny bit of sodium fluoride in the fantastic and precise proportion of one part to a million parts of water for tooth preservation? In the end Mayor Bunton contended that we were fiddling with Mother Nature herself and we'd all get our faces slapped if we kept it up.

Dr Hogan, the superintendent of the Albury Base Hospital, looked rattled and the No men shuffled in their seats as the auditorium seemed to be enthralled by the silver tongues against the fluoride. Dr Hogan produced a chart prepared by the Albury Dentists' Association. He used a red pointer but no one could see the chart through the smoke. It fell on deaf eyes. The dentists had got their heads together and worked out that fluoridation in Albury would save 5000 children's teeth. That, he explained, meant 5000 individual teeth, not 5000 children, because there were only 11,000 people in the town anyway. It could be as high as 8000 teeth, he explained. That was surely a boon for large families hit hard by Menzies Bloody Credit Squeeze. Even though fluoridation could cost £5000 to set up and £2000 per annum, these costs were offset by allowing the saving of three teeth per family which translated to a cost of £3. He was hoping to hit the hip pocket nerve.

But Dr Hogan lost the Civic Theatre that night when he said that the Albury lay public was ill equipped to judge such health measures. Dad lifted his crossed arms higher on his chest and stuck one of his chins out. Someone yelled out that the referendum cost more than £2000 and that it was money down the drain. Like fluoride, countered Mr Harding in his north Queensland accent. Fluoride was only 10 shillings a person a year, Dr Hogan went on, but the next speaker's technical argument was beyond the reach of his largely dentured audience. Dr Stern, who extracted one of my left molars incorrectly when he had the x-ray back to front but later pulled the right one free of charge, described the growth pattern of children's teeth. Teeth with disease fell out early and new teeth forced up prematurely grew without guidance and pointed every which way leaving the mouth looking like the headstones in a deserted country town cemetery.

The reply from the No side was withering and powerful. Alburnians should have the freedom to choose whether or not to let their teeth rot. It was a God-given right. The body was the Tabernacle of God. We should treat it accordingly. I wasn't very house proud to begin with. Fluoride was responsible for poisoning the body. It caused dry births in New Zealand, cancers in America, gall stones in mice, milk dried up in cows, black teeth in Great Britain, cumulative poisonings around the world, thyroids burst in Toledo, dentists in fluoride-ridden Yass used tank water for domestic purposes rather than the town supply, pillow slips rotted in the laundry, sore mouths in Hastings, dried-up mouths, throats, lips, sores, no saliva, cramps and nausea in the stomach, and holes appeared in containers containing small quantities of fluoride. It was a parent's right to choose their children's education and what was good or bad for them.

Alderman Roach was unstoppable. Corrosion of the water pipes could not be discounted, leading to ratepayers forking out yet again. Some people were allergic to it. Who were they? How could you tell? It would be too late when the fluoride was in the water supply and down the gullet and blowing up the vital internal organs.

Finally the crowd responded with a spontaneous eruption of clapping when a teacher stood up during question time and said we already drank our own bath water as people swam in the Waterworks below the Weir at Mungabareena and this water was pumped directly into the town reserve. We drank not only our own bath water but our neighbours'. What it had to do with fluoridation nobody knew but it sure sounded fine, especially as everyone knows that everyone else wees in the water upstream at the Mungabareena Waterworks.

The audience escaped the Civic ready to vote early and to vote often if necessary. Dad guided the Holden into our back yard and Mum shussed the kids upstairs to bed. The front doors were closed against the night but the bar burst into song at the sight of Dad and it was I'll take you home again Kathleen to where your heart is fresh and green until early morning. The shunters, mill workers, shift workers and the shiftless all joined in the chorus. Dad beckoned me behind the bar and I served my time until I was so tired I fell asleep at the tap.

Before doing so I served according to the instructions of the night. Dad had put Corio

Australian whisky into the Red Johnny Walker Scotch bottle through a plastic funnel as part of his morning duties. The Red Johnny Walker went into the Black Johnny Walker bottle. If a customer ordered a full Scotch and dry ginger ale, then after a couple it was Corio at Scotch prices and then after a couple more just plain dry ginger. Amazingly, they still got extremely pissed just on the soft drink and it's for their own good you know. Ernie Carpenter, who if you remember lost his right arm shunting while drunk, then got a desk job at the railway but lost the other arm while crossing the rails late one night going home from the pub, held his drink in two hooks. It took less liquor to get him drunk since he lost his arms, less to go around. He smoked cigarettes the way a schoolgirl pretends to with a pencil. He always dipped his hat to Mum with one of his claws holding the brim. Evenin' Mrs Street. She said he was a gentleman to his fingertips. He glanced left and right if someone swore in front of a lady. Which cunt said fuck, he cried out once in a rage.

From the street the bar windows glowed a dirty pale brown, dark and eerie. Slurred songs of sadness lost their voices as they staggered up the street. Big Jeff Eames rode home on his bike like a huge Russian bear with a half dozen bottles under his arm. A Mack truck could hit him front on but those bottles wouldn't break in his grip even if he lost a limb or two. He'd beaten the gambling bug and his weakness for poker machines by barring himself from the RSL club. They wouldn't let him rejoin even when he promised to fight in the next two wars.

Mum sat on a barstool behind the bar over the cellar door sipping a shandy and chatting with a customer. The regular boarders competed silently with each other to be the last one leaving and travelling salesmen eagerly watched the back door for signs of womenfolk. The pool table players tried to keep the sound down by hitting the cue ball gently. Potato chips were crunched quietly. No bother. The police hardly worried us while we awaited the appeal. They felt they'd gone too far. A man's got to earn a living. I blew my nose into a tea towel before drying up some glasses. No one noticed. Tomorrow was another day but it was already tomorrow and I went to bed and to school next morning smelling of beer, cigarette smoke, peanuts and urine.

Seven potato

Dr Mackenzie's motorised anti bed-wetting device was thankfully only AA-battery operated but guaranteed for twelve months. It had come by seamail from the USA, ordered by Dad through a coupon in a men's magazine. It was an electric blanket in reverse. If moisture touched any part of the patent-pending undersheet, a clock would explode into alarm mode via the mass of wires threaded throughout and hanging from all sides. It would wake the dead to the world, even those about to urinate, who were then expected to pull their heads in and make for the toilet and complete matters.

However, I was trained to ignore early morning alarms, train sounds, highway honks from the road in front of the pub, late night carousing in the bar below, Mum and Dad snoring. Awoken by the alarm, they came in to see me sleeping soundly in a pool and tangle of wet sheets. Mum stripped the bed while I hung over Dad's shoulder like a long footy scarf. Mum eased off the pungent pyjama bottoms and Dad laid me to rest in a cradle of itching blankets. My pretend sleep soon became real. They whispered over me that the Mackenzie Sensor could be rigged to give short electric shocks which might work better. My sleeping face grimaced like a condemned boy.

Dad talked not so softly of getting the boarders these Mackenzies to save laundry costs. Boarders' sheets were changed weekly unless wet. Grown-up men weed like babies under the drink. My mind jumped around like a pinball machine. How could the Mackenzie distinguish between sweat on a hot summer's night and piss? What if I had one of those wet dreams Taillight told me about? Would I frizzle and fry like a PMG linesman or the golfer who died under a tree at the Bonegilla Golf Course when struck by lightning? I'd rather stay off liquids for a while than risk electrocution. I'd stick to number twos.

Bedwetting was a major embarrassment, a family secret that only the hotel staff, immediate family and the Mackenzie Distribution Group in the USA knew. Katherine Ann, John and Peter didn't do it. The Hood could be counted on to wet his bed every couple of nights. He was four. I was eleven.

The rubbing was confined to a select and secret inner circle of one. Bedwetting would be a no-no at boarding school. I couldn't take Mum's make-up mirror or the tartan cushion for the rubbing to school. I'd have to make do. Use my imagination. Close my eyes. Make a fist of it.

Mum's drinking was a family secret confined to a circle the size of Antarctica but we never spoke of it. It was a given. The thing not said. When I ran messages to Florence's Chemist to get her tablets, camouflaged with orders of Kleenex tissues, tampons and jelly beans, all black if in stock, it was just another errand. But we – me, Katherine Ann, John and Peter – were kind of drug couriers between the pharmacy and Mum. She had seasonal changes of medication. In summer it was handfuls of Relax-a-Tabs; autumn, Bex; winter, Veganin and in spring, Vincent's powders. Dad tried cutting the account so we wouldn't be able to get endless supplies but Mum's fingers desperately found coins in the back corners of drawers, piled them in stacks into our tiny hands and sent us off ostensibly on a message. Dad threatened the chemist physically by lifting him off the ground by his white lapels with one of his huge trout-spotted fists. But there were other chemists and children ready to walk miles for their Mum. Dad couldn't threaten every pharmacist in Albury, Wodonga or the new satellite town of Lavington.

Mum was so pleased on our return, gulping down half a dozen at a time with a sip from the glass of Steradent water still holding her gasping full set of dentures. Mum's cycle was as predictable as Lennox Walker's long-range weather forecasts. Abstinence begat shandies, begat beer, begat brandy, begat pills, begat bed, begat hospital. Then it begat all over again. We never blamed her, not even when the Hood had to go for ray treatment to Wagga Wagga for his birthmarks and Mum made the car stop reaching for the flask of brandy in her pink brunch coat – just one last drink before she herself went to another hospital in Wagga Wagga for nerve treatment. She was not a drunk like the others at the pub. They were drunks. She was sick. She was Mum. We were mum.

During school term the Earth spins slowed; they turned quicker during holidays. It's fast forward in summer holidays and slow motion during school. That's a known fact. Tuesdays brought Latin. Really an extra religious lesson thrown in until Caesar's wars were opened up for us. Everyone knew I was off to Sydney next year and the Unchristian Brothers made extra efforts to ensure I wouldn't embarrass them after I left. Brother Farrell called on me nearly every period to answer something and in a way it had some effect because I took what Dad called hotelwork more seriously and drew squares, circles, maps, wrote Latin sentences and worked out logarithms, hunched over his work desk with the green lamp upstairs in our flat. Before long, would you believe, I was actually enjoying hotelwork, using a ruler neatly, different coloured pens and pencils and even reciting Latin roots. My place in the order of merit in class shot up like Bernborough.

I was still bedwetting and indulging in the rubbing but my brain seemed to be growing so much that I thought I might have to put a brick on it. Mum was mid-cycle but you'd never know it. At school I was still class clown, my underarm farts cracked everyone up and my Father Bongiorno was so real I could've heard confessions. But that Esler was the real McCoy. He once asked Brother Farrell in front of class where girls have the blackest and curliest hair. We all sniggered like brats. Brother Farrell said he didn't know. Esler helped him by saying it had four letters. We were biting our tongues so hard it was lucky most of us had few teeth. Brother Farrell was stumped. Fiji said Esler with the straightest of straight faces. Every so often we asked Brother Farrell to show us Fiji on the map. He never twigged why we all sniggered.

Some kids had already started on the fluoride project. They were consches – the types who covered their schoolbooks in brown paper with holy cards glued on the covers. My project needed a gestation period so I gave the matter no thought whatsoever until the night before it was due. I was in such a panic the project was doomed to be stillborn. There wasn't a *Women's Weekly* in the whole hotel. Not a photo of the Weir, teeth, fluoride or even Cleaver Bunton. King's newsagency was closed so not even a coloured piece of cardboard could be had. A carefully sawed cardboard beer-box side would have to do, even though Fosters Lager seemed to have little to do with fluoride at first blink. Jimmy B offered to paint it blue and did so with bits of cigarette ash and tobacco stuck under the blue smears of drying paint. The usual *methode projecte* was to clag some cut-out pictures on to the cardboard and, using a ruler, join them with arrows suggesting some causal connection. In the absence of any photographs and without any ability to draw, the project looked doomed. A blue cardboard beer-box side would not pass as even an absurdist comment on fluoride. Procrastination had again got me into trouble – but now wasn't the time to think about it.

The Hood was losing his baby teeth as fast as Dad was losing his hair. We called Dad Friar Tuck behind his huge back. He reckoned the bald spot on the top of his head was caused by lifting the cellar door from below with it. Sure thing. In the back tool shed I got the Hood to open his mouth after learning he had already cashed in some fallen teeth with the Tooth Fairy. There were tons of teeth in there with some fleshy gaps. He wouldn't miss one and, as I pointed out, they grow back. John ambled in and reckoned the Hood should get some advance because if I plucked one then the Hood would be out of pocket. A shilling tops. Two bob and done. John and the Hood would split it.

The pliers in Jimmy B's toolbox were too big for the Hood's mouth and there was debate about which one would go. John insisted on symmetry and we agreed on the left eye tooth to even up the lost right one. Mrs Westie's scissors were too slippery but Mum's nail clippers were just what the dentist ordered. In next to no time I had the Hood's tooth in Tarzan's Grip and stuck in place at the top of the blue beer-box board.

The general idea was to follow the flow of decay without fluoride. Not that I was an advocate, just a student. The single tooth represented untreated water, dental fallout without fluoride. But the project needed more colour, more movement, more *teeth*!

Mum kept a spare set of dentures in the drawer next to her side of the bed. A boy could find anything in there and did. If you took everything out at once and tried to put it back in, it would never fit. It was another Black Hole for lost objects. She never wore these dentures; maybe they didn't fit any more, the drink could have shrunk her mouth. I got one of Dad's big white hankies and separated the dentures from the rosary beads, matches, needle and thread, pill wrappings, saints' relics, religious medals and coins. Wrapping the teeth like a fresh fish I snuck into the tool shed where I glued them to the bottom of the cardboard. The best position was to open them like a shark's mouth.

There was still something missing. Aunt Faith had a saying: teeth do not grow on trees, apples do. So I printed that and glued an eaten browning apple core to one side. The project was taking shape. I later learnt it was what was called a collage. At the time it was just a project without pictures. The toothbrush stuck easily, bristles out. Suddenly I clicked my bitten inky fingers. In the photograph album there was a photo Mum took of Dad without his teeth in, mouth wide open, gums like pale sand dunes. All that was needed was a couple of ruled lines explaining the objects and abracadabra, the fluoride project was ready to be placed in a tea towel and nursed carefully, resting on my bare knees, on the school bus the next morning.

Brother Farrell was not overly impressed. The apple had gained a lot of colour overnight. Hayden Sir Sir Livermore won as usual. My Tooth, The Whole Tooth And Nothing But The Tooth wasn't even a place-getter but Taillight thought it was great even though he didn't get it.

More

D ad became a convert to the Top 40 when singer Johnny Horton came on the scene. He began following the ups and downs of the latest singles published weekly by Mid-States Radio Melody Bar in the young people's section of the *Border Morning Mail*. One of his favourites was *Sink the Bismarck*, and everybody in the pub knew the words backwards because Dad would keep slipping out from behind the bar and putting coins from the till into the jukebox until he ran out, and then he'd open the back of it with the key and press the numbers for free. For a while people would not exchange pleasantries but greet each other with a bar or two of *Sink the Bismarck*. In the year of 1941, The War had just begun, The Germans had the biggest ships, They had the biggest guns.

The jukebox revolutionised life in the Ladies Lounge. For a shilling you could hear the latest and greatest on demand. They were queuing up when it was first installed. Fights broke out and sometimes bumped the record off, which only raised tempers further. If Dad didn't have a key it would have been a real moneyspinner.

On Friday nights, if there was no live country and western singer in the beer garden, I'd place ten 45s, 33s or 78s on to the stereophonic hi-fi phonogram upstairs and it would blast through the loudspeakers over the green cement beer garden with tables and chairs pushed out of the way to make a dance floor, encouraging feet to tap and cigarette-holding hands to clap while the Big Bopper, Little Richard, Frank Sinatra and Dean Martin without Jerry Lewis sang their hearts out to Albury's finest dancers.

It wasn't all wine, women and song. They spoke of the referendum over the din and there didn't generally seem too many for it. Not with the Communists, the foot rot, rust and corrosion undoubtedly due to the fluoride. The real voting was to be done here in Dad's Caribbean-flavoured beer garden with multi-coloured lights strung from the walls to the fence.

Mrs Robinson came on Friday nights with her handwritten pamphlets warning of the dangers of fluoride. She rode her bicycle from pub to pub, handing out pieces of butcher's paper cut oblong and each personally written in pen by Mrs R as she couldn't afford printing or stencilling and photo-copying not yet invented. She had such a good hand for writing they looked like facsimiles. During the late fifties she'd written identical pamphlets on the A-Bomb. She was Albury's first protester. Dad kidded she was always peddling something if he saw her bike leaning against the post outside the pub. She singlehandedly turned many swinging voters. Which way was hard to say. She tied her dress around her waist to prevent tangling with the chain and gears. She taught Albury's budding musicians the piano part-time, and we expected a young Liberace any tick of the clock.

Grandma Poppa Monahan lived with Aunt Charity around the corner. Grandpa Eugene Monahan had died earlier in the year, from fluid loss I suspect. He spent his last years in the back sleepout hunched over a giant jam tin for the phlegm from his lungs and nose, a jam jar for his urine and a wet white handkerchief over his sad sick head. He tried to keep a fluid balance with frequent large bottles of beer but lost the battle in the end. He had been a railway fettler with the New South Wales government railroads most of his life, laying tracks all over the south of the State. The prospect of his beloved 4'8" gauge creeping over the Mighty Murray into Victorian hands might have been the final nail in his sleeper. Poppa had never drunk while Grandpa was alive but she made up for it afterwards with my very frequent deliveries of corked white wine first in beer bottles and then in half-gallons she kept under her bed with the chamberpot.

Aunt Charity worked at the pub from time to time. She took five weeks off every year to go on holidays to Kings Cross where she encountered a particularly weird emotion called Kings Cross loneliness which is being alone in the midst of millions of people. Charlie, it's different from being alone in Albury. It's much lonelier. Why do you go then? I need it. Why would you punish yourself like that? You will one day.

Grandpa Monahan's funeral was my first. Father Bongiorno wore a black surplice and I knew I would miss Grandpa's moist blue smiling Irish eyes as much as the shilling tips he gave me to put on a bet. He came from a line of Irish potato famine exiles. His folks were out of Limerick and he sang *It's a long way to Tipperary* between coughing fits.

Poppa kept the big round dial of the Bakelite radio on the ABC in the hope of catching Mayor Bunton upon whom she had a not-so-secret crush. One of Nature's Gentlemen, Cleaver Bunton could have cut a swathe through the Country Women's Association evenings had he been so inclined. Aunts Faith, Hope and Charity were all in love with him.

He could have left his slippers under any of their beds.

Mum could take him or leave him. She only had eyes for Dad and Chateau Tanunda. The run-up to the referendum had taken its toll on Mum and we'd again found bottles of brandy hidden under the sink next to the Pine-O-Cleen and Ajax. Dad frequently audited the bedroom so Mum sought refuge in the kitchen. She was like blotting paper that reached a saturation point and needed to be replaced in order to make sense of what was written. Her days were getting shorter, her nights longer. As the third term went by she spent more time under the kangaroo-skin doona, breakfast, lunch and dinner in bed uneaten, words slurring, getting up to go to the toilet or timidly joining in the late night festivities in the back bar. Katherine Ann would tend to Mum's needs, pulling a brush through her long hair while she nodded off with an inch or two of ash at the end of a cigarette. The Hood no longer slept between Mum and Dad. Dad sometimes slept out the back. Something was happening. Something bad. We never knew. We didn't want to. Maybe it would all go away and Mum would come back from Mount St Mary's Hospital in Sydney with the cure and mother us all to death.

Being first-born bestowed certain duties and obligations like making sure that any jobs I was given were delegated down the line through Katherine Ann to the Hood, after he stopped crawling and began to toddle. I was a great one for delegating, but being an even greater procrastinator I put off delegating so long that I ended up doing the job myself, or putting it off till later. One of the biggest disappointments of my life so far occurred when I obtained my birth certificate to send to the boarding school for the next year. They must have needed proof I was alive, kicking and Catholic. One day I found myself walking down Dean Street on the way home from the Registry of Births, Deaths and Marriages with a sealed copy of my birth certificate. I wondered if they were in some sort of significant order – like Marriage should be before Death I think. Anyhow, I checked out my date of birth, 17 July, great day, and place of birth: Albury Hospital, opposite Hoyts Picture Theatre.

Then suddenly, out of the blue, it hit me square between the eyes. In the same year I was born my parents had married on 3 January. Oh my God! How could they have done that? Why wasn't I told? It's my life! I started to jog towards the pub to confront Mum and Dad. A child should be told the circumstances of his birth. Married in January. Born in July. I deserved to know, but I found out this deep family secret accidentally. I was born three months premature and I never even knew! I was a premmie of six months. For eleven years I'd been walking or crawling around thinking I was a Cancer when all the time I was a latent Libran. Even the fortune teller at the Show was misled. It now all made sense. I wasn't hard on the outside, soft inside like a crab. I did walk sideways when agitated, but I was Libran and proud of it, or a Virgo or a Leo.

Marching into the bar I thrust the certificate in front of Dad. You should have told me. What? This. I pointed to the dates. It's nothing to be ashamed of, Chilla. He called me Chilla when he was in that mood. I hated it. Ashamed? I didn't know and I should have. Don't tell your mother, she's got enough to worry about. He rolled his eyes upwards to the flat like aces in a poker machine. He gave me a lemonade in a schooner glass with crushed ice. Then he said the strangest thing. Chilla, don't blame us. We didn't know how to tell you that you were a bastard. I'd been called a number of things but after that even Chilla sounded all right. Nothing more was said. Mum's the word. If you look hard enough you can see me in their wedding photos.

Kevin Arnold, the supervising shunter, asked me to go and bundy his card off and slipped me a shilling. I looked around to see if anyone else in the bar wanted to knock off work. It was about fifty yards uphill to the railway station which was too far for Kevin and the likes of him. Easier to get me to get their cardboard work cards and bundy them into the machine which stamped the exact time of start up and knock off for payroll purposes. The railways were forever instigating new methods to keep the efficiency of the rail system and the Bundy machine surely revolutionised things. I'd never had so much money. Money for jam. All I did was collect a shilling a head and bundy their cards. Sometimes on and sometimes off, depending on the shift, while they never left the warm snuggle of their barstools. The railways ran like clockwork. It was the job of your life, for your life.

The bottom fell out when the cursed standard gauge went through Albury. Thousands in the town were dismissed. The pub's takings halved then quartered. Dad opened later and later to keep things going. The police charged him. Black marks appeared on his liquor licence. Business was down and his licence in jeopardy but we sang If you ever go across the sea to Ireland, Then maybe at the closing of the day until sun-up sometimes. The coal shovellers and engine drivers dreamt of electric trains. Ernie longed for his lost limbs and again holding the missus, travellers imagined the completion of Albury Aerodrome and Dad shook off thoughts of 24-hour liquor licences and gave in to the Go on Bills and sang *The Foggy Foggy Jew*.

Nine potato

Saturday afternoon saw a stream of punters going between Mr Stephens' house and the pub. A bystander could be fooled into thinking the Stephens place was a shithouse. In the spring air the Saturday afternoon litany played over the radio: They're off at Werribee. A beautiful start with the favourite jumping perfectly in front... I knew every Melbourne Cup winner and the lineage of all the gallopers in Sydney and Melbourne. Dad bought a horse, Court Carey, that turned out to be a fair performer, running second in some important local races including the Holbrook Cup. But we had been unable to track down where Court Carey came from motherwise so the near-winning framed pictures in the Saloon Bar read By Carey out of an unknown dam. Now Court Carey was a real bastard. Carey had run third in the Melbourne and that's as close to stallion royalty as you get in Albury.

For big races Dad would get his special jockey up from Melbourne, Vic Hartman, who'd won a Melbourne Cup when he was younger but in older age loved the sauce a bit too much. On the night before race day Dad had to lock Vic's bedroom door out the back to keep him in and sober until the race was over. Otherwise he could hardly stay on a stool, let alone a horse. You could hear his little fists on the door of room 11 way into the night until he fell asleep, exhausted but painfully sober.

The turf was in our blood and in Mum's lungs. If Court Carey was running that week you could cut the air with any one of Mrs Westie's kitchen knives. We drove up to Culcairn for the Culcairn Cup in the Holden in nervous silence, pulling Court Carey in a trailer behind us. If a town didn't have a racecourse it was nowhere. Even Wodonga had one. Dirt, but Albury's had green grass up most of the straight and on some of the turns. Mum had a new frock from Farrah's House of Fashion and a spring carnival flower hat so wide that we couldn't see the road in front from the back seat.

Frank Duffy had trained the Court to perfection and to the second. Dad had pockets of pound notes wrapped in rubber bands ready for the big stable plunge taking the course bookies by surprise. He tapped his pockets, checking, all the way to Culcairn. Dad parked in the Owners, Trainers and Members parking paddock and I led the Court into the stables, where Frank Duffy grabbed the bridle and took over.

Bush bookies are not known for their bravery, and every one of the ten Cup runners was at odds of less than 5 to 1. The Court was at evens with two other runners. A stable plunge had to be organised well in advance. An owner couldn't get set with a bookie in one bet but had to disperse it among anonymous punters who could all catch the book-makers' ring with their pants down and the Court's odds up. There was no one more anonymous than Captain Jack Saunders (retired) and Jack Davies. Dad slipped them a wad each behind the Members Portable Toilet. We got all our bets on at just under odds on. The Court wasn't even the favourite. It's no wonder Culcairn bookmakers are among life's lottery winners.

The other mark of being one of life's lottery winners was to own a string of racehorses. Some had three or four running in the one race at Cul-cairn. Life's lottery winners look after each other a lot. The big trick of the track punting, Dad told me was to see if the trainer's wife or mother or auntie backed his horse. You had to watch the Totalisator's lines closely and sidle up carefully and hope to hear her place the bet out of the side of your ear.

Vic Hartman rode the Court a treat, there was no chance of getting caught up in the starting wire as Vic had him two lengths behind the starting line when the gun went off. The judges' verdict was a short half head and a yard past the post the Court was well in front. There was no each-way betting at the Culcairn betting ring odds, and Mum kept all the losing tickets in her handbag for luck and keepsakes.

Vic was very thirsty after the race with all the dust. The Court had to come from behind the field and after the last race we all studied the print of the photo finish, trying to work out which horse was the Court in all the dust. Vic took the defeat bad, and sat on the high stool drinking lots of long glasses of beer. From winning the Melbourne Cup to losing the Culcairn Cup is really belittling to a jockey as proud as Vic. There was plenty of room in the back seat for him with us five kids on the way home. He slept most of the way on my lap.

On the Stephens' supersonic stereo radio we listened to the Albury Spring Cup broadcast. In between races the Anti- and Pro-Fluoridation committees had paid advertisements pushing their particular side and reasons for voting yes or no. The No campaign was miles ahead, undoubtedly because Mayor Bunton's voice sounded better than Charlton Heston's in *The Ten Commandments*. Even if he was reading the Albury and District telephone directory, he sounded like you'd think God would if He ever opened up. The Mayor's voice certainly showed up the race callers, whose microphones were on their left because they spoke out of the sides of their mouths. But the race caller was respected for his memory and his way with words. Fields of 20 or more horses, eight times a day, without a mistake. Pure poetry, said Dad. When Time and Tide won the Doncaster, Ken Howard described the finish as Time and Tide sweeps to the lead and Time and Tide waits for no man. But Mayor Bunton had your Churchillian voice with a touch of the bush. No one could say Yackandandah, Mullindollingong, Cootamundra and Burrumbuttock in the same sentence the way he could. Fluoride was a pushover. The right to liberty, the right to our Christian values, the right to say No. Thus spake Bunton. The Yes Committee advertisements used a dentist. They might be good with the rest of the mouth but they're not much good with the tongue. Dentists were called doctors for some reason best known to their wives and Dr Stern, our dentist, sounded like the electric drill he used with relish and without water.

The vote was a week away and both sides had stepped up the momentum with paid radio ads, posters and there was talk of a television advertisement on the Shepparton station. Throwing good money after bad, said Aunt Faith. The radio ads were smartly placed, in the middle of race day, when the whole town was listening. I went home to get my swimming togs. It makes you think, said Jimmy B from his stool in the Public Bar. He had Saturday off work at the pub and thought it was the greatest thing in the world to spend your day off at the pub, drinking in the bar, helping Dad clean up, just like he did on the days he worked. His annual holidays were spent the same way. Dad said he worked slower on his days off but Big Jeff Eames claimed it was too close to call.

Mum was in bed, door closed, curtains drawn, eyes open. I wandered into Taillight's, scaring the shit out of the punters when I let the spring wire screen door go. People were studying the newspaper form guides Scotch-taped to the back wall and running their fingers along the horses' names to check the jockeys and the weights. We agreed to go down to the pool which had just opened for the season. It was semi-final time for the football and the pool had just been refilled after winter and you could lay on the buffalo grass all day at this time of year and not get too sunburnt.

Mum had bought me this floral tropical cotton coloured summer outfit that she'd made me wear to the pictures. I looked like the set in a Tarzan film but the shorts were fine so I had put them on and some sandals and we flicked our towels at each other all the way down Smollett Street to the Olympic Pool.

Taillight was your physical-type person and if you happened to flick him you paid dearly for it with a huge flick back and a chinese burn on your wrist to boot. I tried to make sure my flicks missed my miles but not being a good shot I reached the pool with both my forearms pulsing red.

Smollett Street was part of the Hume Highway joining Sydney and Melbourne with tar and wool trucks zoomed past with great hessian bales of compressed wool for the Farmers and Graziers Store. We stood at the side of the road, as close to the tip of the tar as we could, and waited while the big trucks raced past with such speed that we were windswept off our feet and almost airborne. Then we did it again.

Taillight got closer to the trucks than I ever could. I felt specially vulnerable in my banana and tropical fruit shorts and leather sandals but Taillight lived and breathed danger. It was his middle name. It was the gambler in his blood on both sides. Sometimes I'd fake a lift-off and although Taillight knew he never blew my cover. Just being with him gave me a vicarious, dangerous thrill. With each passing truck he'd edge closer and closer, daring them to brush the red sandy hair that grew in patches over his body. You're a scaredy cat! he barked, picking himself off the gravel by the road-side. The drivers either joined in our game or swerved over the centre line, startling weekend drivers coming the other way.

Taillight had this daredevil-may-care attitude that suggested to those who didn't know him he was slightly unhinged. This was a misconception. He was completely bonkers. His favourite trick was to lie down, face up, in the middle of the train track while the train was in the station, and let the steam blow all over him, and watch the bottoms of carriages run over the top of him. He dared me, double dared me to join him but I never had the heart or Dad the insurance for that sort of thing.

We stopped outside the Farmers and Graziers Store and breathed in that unique mixture of grease, shit, daggy wool, shearers' sweat and hessian that filled the storeroom as much as did the thousands of compressed bags of wool resembling a pirates' fort. We climbed up and fell down five or six storeys of tight wool bags, worked up a sweat diving into unsewn half-filled hessian bags of wool, and then ran down the street as thirsty and as mad as Burke and Wills towards the pool.

In order to get in you had to wait in a queue a mile long to buy special tokens the size of two-shilling pieces costing two shillings to put into a mechanical arm that let you into the pool. Guess it gave someone a job but it seemed pretty superfluous to me. Taillight jumped the barrier even though he'd got a token. Just for the practice, he winked. I dropped mine in but got the wind taken straight out of me when I tried to barge tummy first through the barrier. Red from embarrassment and the lack of oxygen I smiled and sniffed huge gulps of air through my Farmers-and-Graziers-allergy-to-wool-inflamed nostrils.

Taillight had no inhibitions as proved in his Dad's Humber and slipped his togs on in front of everyone on the sewerage treatment plant side of the pool. I wrapped a towel completely around me, sat down and wriggled into mine. I liked to take to the water in stages, through the wading pool with my feet, warm with gallons of baby piss, where the sun only needed to reach out about a foot to touch the bottom. Then into the shallow end, down a step at a time on the aluminium ladder into the water.

Taillight did a bomb from the springboard at the deep end, right into the faces of some girls sitting on the tiled side dangling their feet into the water. He was a mad bomber from way back. Each one was at least the equivalent of the Bikini Atoll blast. On the Richter scale at the baths his high tower bomb with pike was a nine or ten. Sunbathers on the buffalo grass outside the wire fence were sprinkled with far-flung drops of chlorinated water and stood cursing at the carrot-topped bomber flailing his arms like windmills in the water. I pretended to some I didn't know him and admitted to others that we were together. It was tough on me knowing whose side I was on.

We raced each other across the width of the pool. Sometimes I beat him but then I was on land running alongside the pool while he did freestyle in the water. Dad had paid Mr Roxborough £2 a lesson for me last summer. After about four over-arms my body felt completely buggered. I couldn't kick at the same time, chlorine caused my nose to run pure phlegm, and my eyes stung as if sprayed with Mortein insect repellant. I was not cut out to be a fish like Dad who cut through the water like he had an outboard strapped to his back. I was your waterwings sort of boy.

The pool got its water from the Mighty Murray River which curled like a giant draft resister around the pool and down the side of the sewerage treatment works. The Hume Weir was over 600 feet high and any cold water released into the river through its wall came from the very bottom where only monster Murray cods and icebergs survived. When Taillight went swimming in the river he always patted the water around him when he surfaced shouting Where's my balls? Where's my balls? Desperate immigrants from Victoria never waded across the river but snuck along the old Union Bridge. They would not have survived the cold.

Different radio stations from transistors crack-
led out in a Tower of Babel from the tops of towels
laid out on the rough cement and across the buffalo
grass. The sunbathers all pointed in the same direction like napping seals trying to pick up the radio
signals from the top of Monument Hill. Dads
floated upright in bloomers with their circling kicking children. Waterwings kept kids afloat and flip-
pers made them champions – at splashing. Sensitive
types wore ear plugs and the very sensitive had
nose clips. Old women had rubber bathing caps.
Teenage girls squinted at magazines covered in their
fingerprints from Johnson's Baby Oil. Secretaries
took care not to get their Saturday morning hair
wet before Saturday night by going down in the
water only to where their breasts were beginning to
grow. All the cement places were taken so Taillight
and I had left our towels, clothes and sandals in a
bunch in the corner of the fence, hoping for a space
by the time we got out.

There was a great drawback to looking for coins
and stuff at the bottom of the pool as anything you
saw was more likely to be further away than it
looked and usually turned out to be a bottle top.
But the worst thing was the chlorine that made your
eyes burn and look like road maps. Mind you, it
suited Taillight. But I usually searched the bottom
like Helen Keller at the shallow end. With fluoride
in the water as well your eyes might fall out, I told

Taillight. He thought they might neutralise each other but I doubted it.

We lay on our backs, fluttering our eyes at the sun, oblivious that skin cancers were being invented right under our noses. The shrieks, cries, cat-calling, splashing about, shouting and general bally-hoo blended together in an earful like no other. Swimming pool static. Taillight bludged a smoke from someone and held it tight in the crevice of his forefingers, close to his palm. He blows smoke out of his nostrils and rings out of his mouth. Mum swears it comes out of his ears as well. She doesn't know it but I've seen him light his farts with matches, like a blowtorch.

Despite the back seat incident in his Dad's Humber, Taillight didn't strike me as queer, more someone who was up for anything. It didn't worry me at all but I didn't turn my back on him in the changing room afterwards and chose the furthest shower.

The day was still a pup. The sounds of squealing and splashing echoed through the changing shed like an auditorium. Taillight suggested we run by Norieul Park on the way home where sometimes he said if you were very lucky gypsies camped and sunbathed in the nude. You're kidding me, I said. There was a hole in the fence at the back of the baths behind the treatment works which allowed you access to the sports ground where Albury were playing a grudge match against Wodonga.

It was three-quarter time and Fred Goldsmith the burly full forward late of the Melbourne League was standing in a huddle with the other Albury Tigers making out how he could wipe out the defeat in the last quarter. The Albury Tigers had their very own footy jumpers which were exact replicas of the Big League's team Richmond who were also called the Tigers, black with a yellow diagonal stripe across the front and back, like a communion sash. Some of the young players wore sleeveless jumpers showing off their timber-cutting, fence-posting muscles. Not Freddy Goldsmith who'd peaked a few years earlier in the Big League and was playing out his time in the Ovens and Murray League until he could get a coaching job back in the Big Smoke. He was captain and coach of the Tigers and as an ex-Melbourne player was viewed with a bit of awe by the locals. There was a certain captain's swagger in his collapsed socks, the way he held his cigarette cupped inside his hand and close to his lips and blew smoke out of the side of this mouth while revving up his players and occasionally sipping from a small bottle of beer. It was little wonder that the Wodonga Bulldogs had us on the run. The bottom had fallen out of the Tigers and the Bulldogs had that small-town-beats-city smell of blood in their wet nostrils. None of them smoked or drank beer during three-quarter time.

Footy was getting professional these days. An occasional Come on the Tigers! burst out of the grandstand but mostly it was advertisements over the loudspeaker system. So as not to interrupt the flow of play announcements were not broadcast during the game but read one by one during each quarter break, kiddies were lost and found, Pinky from Tumut was at the Sportsmen's Bar waiting for Mr McGregor from Tumut, scores in other games were read out, leading to ohs and ahs around the ground, and the latest race results and starting prices updated and forthcoming festivities and activities highlighted.

Taillight scored us two pies with sauce, too hot for me to do much but nibble the sides while he gulped his down piping hot. It must be something to do with his red hair and real sense of invincibility. My brown hair and burnt lips seemed to go hand in hand. After the ball up and a couple of Go the mighty Tigers there was a Bulldogs goal and we left in case we cursed them some more.

You could follow the river's edge to Norieul Park or cut through a couple of paddocks and hit the alleged Hovell Tree and turn right through the caravans and campsites. Menzies Bloody Credit Squeeze saw a drastic increase in vans and tents at the park, with families not just holidaying but actually living there and sending their kids to public school. It sounded kind of fantastic to me, living in a tent by the river with electric cords running in all directions like vines. The people who lived there didn't seem to share this view. A flap over their heads was nothing like a roof and wooden planks on the ground didn't feel like carpet.

Taillight pelted me with a couple of those fluffy but hard seedlings that fall out of plane trees. He had a strong arm and although they'd break up on impact they stung like hell. He'd linger over the cars parked next to the caravans and tents and check them out, pointing out accessories and double gaskets and stuff I couldn't give a hoot about. I was more interested in the people in the cars. Taillight was going through a phase where a comb from a shirt pocket was constantly attending to his hair, carefully making tracks through it and tufting the middle up into a pompadour, which fell forward like a red cockatoo over his forehead. He nudged me to check out some girls in two-pieces playing under the sprinklers on the lawns near the changing sheds. Typical girls, he said, when there's a raging river just at their doorstep.

Norieul Park attracted mostly your Bonegilla migrant families who spread out on army blankets with Eskies full of Tupperware and silver foiled meats of an odd heritage. There was a middle-aged – ie over twenty – secretary or two on long towels reading romantic paperbacks, with a pack of cigarettes and matches carefully placed one on the other. They held their cigarettes in very straight fingers, tapping the ash into the grass as far away from the towels as their arms would allow. Transistors emitted race broadcasts, bits of football and Top 40 hits, depending on their owners' tastes.

Taillight dropped his daks and raced headfirst towards the moving river, throwing black mud up on to tut-tutting mothers who screwed up their faces like rinsing rags. In a plunge he was on to the knotted rope and halfway across the river, almost in Victoria before letting go in a half dive half jump half bomb, arms and legs stuck out as if he were a Swiss Army knife. The splash reached the towels of startled sunbathers who blinked and silently cursed the oncoming rain. The serious had oiled up on the baby oil and clicked their bodies and towels with the heels of their feet around the descending sun like clockwork sundials.

The river cupped Taillight in its wet hands, carrying him around the bend and out of sight for a moment before dropping him in still water near the bank. He raced up shaking his bright red hair like an Irish setter, water drops lingering in the air as if on cobwebs before smacking into those nearby. Jesus the water was cold. My skin broke out in blue goose bumps just from the spray. Russians and Mao Tse Tung would like the Mighty Murray downstream from the Weir but not yours truly or my family jewels.

Taillight shivered and reached into his pants for a tailor-made Turf and box of Redheads to warm him up. He loved a smoke. In fact he looked like a lit cigarette himself. Funny thing about Taillight was that he always looked middle-aged, even as a youth. He must have looked like a teenager when he was born. We sat down on the browning grass, he sucking up the tar and nicotine, holding the smoke in his open mouth, all blue and red, before blowing it out in shaky circles for me to inhale passively beside him. I think I could be seven feet tall if I didn't hang around Taillight or Mum and Dad. Probably get lung cancer with my luck, and not ever have smoked a fag. Taillight offered me one when we were fishing for redfin the year before. Not now, I said politely, intently studying the nylon line for any sign of a tug. He accused me of never having had a fag which of course I denied. We both knew I was lying. Eventually I took one from his packet and he lit it for me. I managed somehow to get it going and when he turned away to check his yabbie traps I flicked the cigarette into the river. He soon came back and asked how I enjoyed it. Great. He asked where the butt was. I pointed to a nearby rock and said I put it under there. He kicked it over. Nothing there. I was as red as him. He never pressed one on me again.

Albury was changing. After the blackfellas were

evicted last century, hundreds of Irish refugees fleeing the lack of potatoes at home found rich soil for the potato-growing by the banks of the Mighty Murray. The shops and solicitors were littered with names like Ryan, O'Shaughnessy, Carrol, Dury, Cornell, Fitzpatrick, Leahy, O'Callaghan and Purtle. At the same time Germans in search of a sense of humour followed a winemaker named Frauenfelder and settled in peace in the Ovens and Murray Valley, in due course marrying into Irish families and breeding generations of children who didn't know whether to raise a fist or a smile. Of course there were always a couple of Lebbos: Maloufs, Dihoods, Saroffs and Batrouneys. But now the spread of Communism saw families with fathers with engineering degrees and names ending in –ski working in timberyards and on the roads and taking all the freckles from Albury's pale skin and turning it olive almost overnight. Taillight blamed Bonegilla and its migrants who set up stakes in the nearest town. Bloody wogs, he called them. We had a few at school. Bloody wogs, I said, not too loud lest I be heard by the gypsy family packing up for the day. I told Taillight how the wogboys couldn't even speak English properly and still seemed to come at the top of the class. Bloody cheats these bloody wogs. Hundreds of them had taken all the best jobs on the Snowy Mountains Hydroelectric Scheme which could have guaranteed a century's work for real

Australians if those Yugoslavs and Italians hadn't come over here and finished the bloody thing off two years ahead of time. Bloody wogs.

If we left now we'd have time to nick into Nana's pub on the way home for a squash. Taillight carefully combed his hair on each side and curled the middle up into a crest before padding the front down on to his forehead. Aunt Faith said he was awfully neat about his hair for someone with truckloads of dirt under his nails.

Nana Waterstreet's pub was called the Pastoral Hotel. Sand-blasted sheep grazed opaquely in the front windows and Nana and Aunt Hope presided quietly over the bar where the customers tended to be more your shopkeeper, your travelling salesman or your public servant. Both women often sat on bar stools inside the bar with pre-goitred chins pressed hard on their aproned chests, licking the fingers of the left hand while turning the pages of the *Border Morning Mail* with the other hand. They ignored customers until they either left in disgust or nearly died of thirst. Profit was not their motive, but routine. Aunt Hope loved the pokies and her right arm made the left look like it was withered. It bulged from the pulling of the pokies.

Womenfolk weren't afraid of going alone to the Pastoral, unlike Waterstreets. However, I'd seen Nana and Aunt Hope throw their weight around if things got out of hand. But with their lack of speed serving behind the bar it was pretty hard for a bloke to get drunk at the Pastoral. Dad reckoned they were secret members of Alcoholics Anonymous. There was never any great rivalry between the family's pubs because they served two very different types of Alburnians. Dad boasted that we owned a chain of hotels.

Taillight and I gravitated to Aunt Hope's end of the bar, where she had two or three cigarettes on the go at once. One for each lung and one for the road. You could tell that Dad's and Nana's hotels were as old as the hills because they had phone numbers still in double or triple digits. The newer businesses had a string of numbers up to four or five, with developments in Lavington and up behind the new Sisters Without Mercy Hospital. Hope was the soft touch, and soon Taillight and I were gobbling potato chips and brushing flakes from our mouths, washed down with thick real lemon squashes. God it was good to be kings in Albury.

Nana beamed at me but frowned at Taillight, him being non-Catholic and rowdy to boot. He was a one-boy crime wave. You spoil that boy, Hope, she said, which only made her spoil me some more. Nana was left with five children by my grandfather, my namesake, when he carelessly departed this life before the Big War, leaving Nana very little in his will. After some court battles she emerged with a keen sense of the penny. She made her own soap, black as Vegemite, and washed the hotel linen with it herself. Most of the Pastoral's travellers packed their own soap from home if they intended a visit.

Nana was complaining about buying a billycart of manure that morning from a local boy for two shillings. It was double the usual cost. She asked the boy why it had doubled. The boy said the price of chaff had doubled. And so it goes, she moaned. Nana had strong views on all matters. It seemed that the less she knew of something, the stronger the position she took. She was puzzled that if homosexuality was inherited, why hadn't it died out?

This fluoride business will be the death of us. Mark my words. Aunt Hope was tut-tutting like a ticking clock, shaking her head, causing the Saturday-night-set hair to wobble under its hairnet as if there was an earthquake. She was reading the rest of the *Border* left over after the race section had been pencilled and inked all over as she built up her piggy bank by betting during the afternoon ready for an assault on the pokies that night at the club. It's poison, that's for sure, confirmed Nana. That Khrushchev and his cronies will stop at nothing. He calls himself peace-loving and explodes A-bombs all over the place. Once they start fiddling with the water it's a hop, step and jump to a dictatorship.

Taillight and I watched like spectators at a tennis match as Nana and Aunt Hope discussed the forthcoming referendum and its fallout. One thing was clear, and that was that fluoride in the water had a snowball's chance in hell at the Pastoral.

Nana's pub attracted the middle classes and even some of life's lottery winners from Forest Hills who didn't drink at the New Albury Hotel or the Albury Club. The bar was full of men in tweed coats with Apex, Rotary or Lions Club pins. They debated things calmly over their half-brandies and gins. Nana was a great charity worker for the local Albury City Band. On a recent bottle drive she had organised over 5000 dozen beer bottles for the cause. Could have been more except for the competition from the cans, she said.

We beat it home before one of the customers did something outrageous like raise his voice or say damn.

Ten potato

At the other end of Smollett Street the atmosphere at Waterstreets Railway Commercial Hotel was very different. Fs and cs hung in the air like Christmas lights, Mr Stephens was settling bets, songs burst out in fits and starts, kids drank raspberries in the back of utes, and Dad was putting out extra tin ashtrays in the beer garden for the Saturday night festivities. The jukebox was choked up with paid requests till Kingdom Come. I cheerioed Taillight at his front gate.

All was well with the world as I climbed the front stairs two at a time. John was playing with matches at the top of the stairs, trying to get two of them to stick together while burning. Mum's door was shut, no light under it. She was asleep, or out cold. The hallway between her bedroom and the lounge was a demilitarised zone. None of us kids lingered there very long, lest we be called for service to the bar or chemist for her. The sun had stirred my skin and the devil plays with idle glands. My mind turned to thoughts of the rubbing, but Katherine Ann was sitting on the tartan cushion plaiting her doll's hair. John, Peter and the Hood could be anywhere. The flat was inhospitable to a boy with some rubbing to do. Maybe it was just as well, because the inevitable guilt afterwards would take the glow off my Saturday night. It's harder than you think to maintain the Augustine Attitude.

Taillight would soon be doing Deanies on his Malvern Star bike with electric lights and white trimmings. He was sure to score, cop a feel. I felt so immature next to him. We were once having a milkshake at the Dairy Queen when two high school girls recognised him and before long he was telling dirty jokes like a trooper. Do you know any, Charlie? one of the girls asked me. I pointed to each of her emerging tits, her crutch and behind in turn with a finger. Milk, milk, lemonade, round the corner chocolate's made. It's a very fine line that a young boy crosses between fart and poo jokes to your actual sex joke, as Taillight pointed out to me later. There's a difference between what makes you kack yourself and what makes them wet their pants.

Taillight was a wizard at the chick chat. After a couple of minutes at the Dairy Queen, chicks were putty in his hands. Under his bright red hair burnt a natural flame that he turned on at will. He may not have been able to speak Latin but he spoke fluent chick in ways I needed subtitles to understand. He flirted the same way he fished. With great success. I could dangle my line right next to his off the old Union Bridge and not get a bite while he pulled redfin after redfin out of the Mighty Murray and into the plastic bucket. Taillight is a legend.

There was a walk-in closet at the end of the hallway with a brass cliplock that you could use once inside. It had enough room on the floor if you moved the cedar trunk underneath Dad's suits and jackets which he only wore to important stuff like funerals, race meetings or court appearances. Mum had left a hand mirror which could be positioned just so. All that was needed was the tartan cushion. Nothing else would do. I had some sort of unnatural crush on it. Pillows, blankets and towels felt weird, like I was being unfaithful. Me and the cushion were kind of going steady. How could I get Katherine Ann off it without drawing undue attention? It was starting to cake and chip a bit, especially on the bottom zipper side. I wondered if Katherine Ann could get pregnant from just sitting on it. I was too young to be a father, especially with my sister. I was too young to be even a son. But there's no use crying over spilt milk.

Katherine Ann didn't know what had happened.

One minute she was plaiting baby's hair, the next it was in the laneway about to be flattened by a Border Transport truck. She let off a cry that threatened to wake the dead to the world but Mum didn't stir. Katherine Ann ran down the stairs screaming blue murder in perfect pitch. Even in hysterics she was capable of hitting notes that would have caused the crystal to break in the bar if we had any.

In one swoop I switched cushions and threw the tartan one into the closet. Dad marched into the flat with the muddy squashed doll in his hand and my sister in tow. It jumped, Dad, I tried to explain. I wasn't born yesterday, he said. Neither was I, obviously. All my family had the knack for the right expression, except Mum who sometimes when angry with me threatened to give me a father of a hiding. Would Dad give me a mother of one?

Like Brer Rabbit I hoped he would lock me in the closet, but after wagging his big tobacco-stained index finger at me he stripped the dirty clothes off the doll and threw them into the clothes basket, leaving the damaged doll nude and Katharine Ann bellowing. She sat down on the couch oblivious to the switcheroo. Dad told her to be quiet, nodding to Mum's room, gave her the hairbrush and retreated downstairs to easier tasks.

I backed slowly into the closet, bolted the door

and while Katherine Ann sobbed outside in inter-
mittent gulps I lay down on the cushion and started
the rubbing in the dark. I wasn't really feeling
myself and couldn't get the image of the naked doll
out of my head. The rubbing was turning me weird.
It didn't even have a pussy, whatever that looked
like. I'd never seen one but had it on good authority
from Taillight that they were desirable. He called
them gashes. He always gave me good advice. If
ever I had a date with a girl, it's the second hole
from the back of the neck. Taillight was so other-
worldly wise.

At the end of the day the rubbing is hardly
worth it. But a boy's gotta do what a boy's gotta
do. It's hard to keep an eye on the door for
intruders, an eye on the mirror, a hand where it
counts and the other moving the cushion around
faking passion. Every bump or far off cough
sounded like the rapping of knuckles on the door.
With my white bum in the air, my shorts around
my ankles, it would have taken more explaining
than even Harry Flood, Albury's only university
qualified lawyer, was capable of. The thing with
the rubbing, even if the bottom was falling out of
it, was that it was a mortal sin even if you only
thought about it. So if you were going to Hell in a
basket just for thinking about it, you may as well
do it. It's not like Hell is one of those gas stoves
with small jets at the front and the big jets at the

back. It's more like Mrs Westie's big wood and coal burning monster stove in the kitchen. If you spit on the edge of it four or five feet away from the flames, it sizzles and the spit steams off in an instant. When Jimmy B cleaned it once a year it took a couple of days to cool down and everything had to be cooked on small outdoor camping gas rings the size of Bunsen burners. There were no grades in Hell. No Black and Gold. It was always exam time, without hope of graduation.

The long and the short of it being that you may as well be hung or burnt for a sheep as a lamb. So do it, don't just think it. The trouble is, sometimes it's hardly worth it. In the dark of the clothes closet you can barely see the mirror without a flashlight and suddenly the rubbing was over, the cushion moistened, before I'd even got up to speed. I was overcome with an immediate sense of guilt and shame. Saint Paul my patron saint of purity frowned and wagged his finger from boxes of holy cards in a shoe box on the top blanket shelf. The black beady eyes of the fox-head stole would have blinked if they could, but instead bored into me. My face would have been as white as the Holy Ghost but for the blushing. God could not only see what I'd done, but he knew about the nude doll thing. There's no hiding place for dirty thoughts. Where's the cut-off point for mortal sin in thinking about sex? Like with stealing, it was £10 – anything less was venial and resulted only in purgatory. Could you think dirty for 10 seconds and then stop? Or do you add up all the thoughts as they come and go? Sometimes the thoughts are sitting around in your head before you know it. Can you be blamed for wet daydreaming? I tried to think of cricket, fishing or the pictures, but they kept coming back. Dirty thoughts have a mind of their own.

I fell out of the closet exhausted and tippytoed into the lounge room, throwing the guilty quilty green tartan cushion under my bum in one movement as I slumped on to the couch. Katherine Ann deliberately ignored me with an angled tilt of her head, humming Silent Night, Holy Night and rubbing spots from the newly-dressed doll's communion robe with a hankie-wrapped finger dipped into the mouth of a bottle of Pine-O-Cleen. John had moved on to his Meccano Set which had grown into some leaning tower of Pisa in the middle of the lounge room with hundreds of green and red struts and platforms and screws and nuts all over the place. Peter watched in awe. The Hood picked his nose, rolled it up tight and swallowed. Another Saturday night at home.

After feasting on Mrs Westie's Saturday night special, burnt curried sausages two veg – ten shillings with all the bread and melted butter and margarine curls you could eat and all the tea or chicory you could drink, with a choice of two

sweets thrown in – I stacked the 45s upstairs in
piles of tens for the beer garden dancing. Dad had
taught me the art of being Mr Music Master of the
Ladies Lounge and Beer Garden, if it wasn't rain-
ing. The more they danced, the thirstier they got.
The thirstier they got, the more they drank. The
more they drank, the more we made. The trick is to
start with the slow stuff, your Rosemary Clooney,
Andy Williams or Pat Boone, then slowly build it
up with Bobby Vee, Elvis Presley and even Bill
Haley and the Comets. By about ten o'clock the
tropical themed beer garden was rocking and rolling under the multi-coloured string of lights that
shorted whenever it rained.

When I set up a new lot of ten on the stereophonic phonograph I'd rush to John and the other
boys' room and peer out over the beer garden
where skirts funnelled out like umbrellas as women
twirled under men's arms, where the lonely and shy
gathered in groups of envy around the side bar, and
bouffant- and beehive-haired wives frowned at their
husbands' dirty jokes. Get out of it, they said. They
secretly memorised them for retelling on Monday to
the neighbours' wives.

Everybody smoked, and when the lights went
out at ten past ten o'clock a hundred points of red
light glowed and waved in the dark from burning
tips. I was Dad's disc jockey and he insisted that
this was the time to put on the really sad stuff, the

country and western ballads of Patsy Cline, Brenda Lee and the songs of heartbreak, the stuff that makes them cry into their beers and want to drown their sorrows with more of the same. You had to keep the sound down low at that time so the cops didn't have some busybody ringing up and complaining and interfering with the arrangements.

Mum was a no-show tonight but I could hear Dad's voice lifting softly from the back bar on the back of a chorus of *Danny Boy*. Dad had a great set of tonsils for a man with double dentures and three packs a day. It was heartbreak hotel until Big Jeff Eames called Time, time gentlemen please, about two in the morning.

Eleven potato

Mr Stephens said he'd take us out shooting to Rutherglen for the day. Mrs Stephens had packed an Esky full of sandwiches, big bottles of beer and soft drinks to wet our whistles. Dad was more than sceptical when I told him that Mum said I could go. I had sort of asked her and sure she may have been asleep at the time, but Dad was really being a bit technical. I argued that she nodded. Nodded off more likely, he replied. Earbashing him in the car all the way down Smollett Street to ten o'clock Mass did the trick and he said he'd let me go if I'd look after Mum that night.

Ten o'clock Mass was not for the faint-hearted or the starving classes because you can't eat beforehand and still go to communion. I reckoned everyone in the church was dreaming of bacon and eggs and toast with butter dripping down the sides. The church had the religious side of business all sewn up. On Saturdays the priests heard confessions in the afternoon, so theoretically by Sunday morning you should still be in a perfect state of grace. Well, you would be if you hadn't snuck off into the clothes closet for a bit of the rubbing the night before. Somehow I now found myself sitting in about the fifth row from the front of the church where everyone in town would see me if I didn't go to communion. Being up the front with all the holy rollers and life's lottery winners like the Carricks and O'Shaunessys, I'd stick out like a sore thumb if I stood up to let the rest of the bench go to the aisle for communion and just sat back down there on my lonesome. They'd know I was not in a fit condition to go to communion. They'd know I was suffering from mortal sin. They'd know that there's not too many mortal sins an eleven-year-old boy could commit. In fact, there's really only one, unless he's a murderer. They'd know I'd been at it, fiddling with myself, committing acts of impurity. They might even know about the doll. Jesus, Mary and Joseph. My crumbling teeth clenched in mortal fear and with the shame of it. My legs started jiggling inside my trousers. A bit of wee wee trickled into my underpants. I nearly stood up and confessed at the top of my voice on the spot. A hopeless and helpless panic had set in.

Father Clancy mounted the pulpit like a confident boxer rushes the ring. He had the gift of the gab and it wasn't a gift he kept to himself. Aunt Faith said he loved the sound of his own voice. His robes in the all green colours of the club with brown cross back and front trailed behind him. Nuggety but as fit as one of the Thursday Islanders on the drum in Jimmy Sharman's Travelling Boxing Show, he barely reached the microphone in his built-up shoes. He stood on his toes to deliver his sermon, touching the side of his nose with a thumb from time to time.

The Holy Father in Rome himself had issued a papal bulletin condemning the use of A-bombs by Russia and asking everybody to pray that the church be restored there to its former glory. More than ever, Catholics must pray together and be in the forefront of the fight against Communism. They had infiltrated the highest offices in the land. They were trickier than cockroaches in the folds of curtains. There may even be one or two here in the church. Everyone's eyes darted left and right and collectively the entire congregation shook its head in personal denial. You can't be too careful. Their methods are notorious and lethal. One Catholic country after another has fallen foul to their evil plague. Already, Red China was pushing south, converting country after country to their heathen gospel at pistol point. They especially punished

Catholics. Let us say a special prayer for those poor suffering souls under the sinister spell of Communism. God made the Heavens and the Earth and He made everything just perfect. Water was a powerful weapon for good but too much of a good thing can lead to drowning death and destruction. God had used water to punish the people of Noah's time. He had manipulated it when He gave Moses the power to part the Red Sea. His son even walked on it when out fly fishing with Peter and the Apostles. But once the government starts fiddling with God's gifts it's the thin edge of the wedge. The floodgates will literally open and we'll all be drowned and lost forever to God and His infinite mercy. Fluoride is one of the deadliest poisons known to man. Why in God's name would you put it in the water? It does not take much of an imagination to see where the Communists could literally wipe out an entire population by secretly overusing the fluoride. If God had wanted fluoride in the water, He'd have put it in. Vote with your heads [forefinger to forehead] not your hearts [forefinger to left chest]. How would you like to bless yourself [fast finger circle] coming in and out of the church with fluoridated holy water, or, worse, baptising little babies [thumbed cross on forehead] with the tainted water, endangering their tiny little bodies while at the same time giving them passports to

Heaven? Fluoride weakens the human willpower and that's where the Communists know the Christian mind can be vulnerable to manipulation and takeover. Their indoctrination powers can make all of us robots, unable to resist their heathen teaching and false promises. With weakened minds throughout the Murray Valley, the Riverina would fall like the dominoes in Eastern Europe and Asia.

Clancy was right, whispered Dad, other towns in New South Wales had started to consider fluoride in their water supplies. He started to count them on each of his enormous fingers: Bombala, Condobolin, Cooma, Forbes, Murrumbarra, Scone, Tenterfield, Wellington, Tamworth and Goulburn. He'd read it in the *Border*. There was talk that Sydney's next. If Albury goes fluoride, the whole State could be red.

All of this had distracted me from my own peculiar predicament, and before you could say Jack Robinson Father Clancy was coming down from the altar with a fistful of communion hosts. Heaven knows why Dad had to sit up the front today of all days. Didn't one of the scribblers and Jesus Christ himself say something about only Pharisees sitting up the front of the church and publicans at the back. Publicans should sit up the back with the tax collectors and the lowest of society. Already there was a row of old people across the front of the altar, on their knees with tongues out like frill-necked lizards, waiting for a piece of the Lord.

Katherine Ann was up like a shot, head bowed, fingers straight as arrows, waiting for me to get up. If I let her go past me I was sunk. Dad raised himself in sections, leaning to the left on the seat in front and then shifting his weight to the other side with an almighty effort, as the bull elephant rises from the African dustpan. It gave me some moments to gather my few wits about me as Dad shook from side to side, half awake, half asleep and the other half reconsidering some of the bets he made the day before. John and Peter were standing now. The Hood was threatening to go even though he hadn't had his own first communion yet.

I began to pray for God's guidance in this time of need and He answered my desperate prayer. A little voice in my head, uncracked and sounding not dissimilar to my own, unveiled the undeniable logic of reason. If I was in mortal sin and didn't go to communion then I was damned anyway if Dad ran the Holden into the giant walnut tree in Smollett Street on the way home. The best I could do was hope to survive the week until next Saturday when I could confess, and risk being in a state of mortal disrepair until then. I'd have to be very careful crossing roads and playing anything with Taillight. But if I went to communion, sure I'd be committing another mortal sin – but could I be in a worse

position than I already was? There are no degrees
of eternity. Hell is all Hell. There's no Saloon Bar.
Hell is Mrs Westie's stove. So I may as well have
another mortal. What the hell's the difference. In
fact it cleared the week for some free and rewarding
rubbing if I could pull this off. Next Saturday I'd
fess up and start all over again. Thank you Dear
God. You never tasted so good, I thought as I
withdrew Him on my tongue back into my gob and
down my throat.

Rutherglen was about 17 miles from Wodonga as
the crow flies down the Murray Valley Highway.
But not many crows were game enough to fly when
Taillight and I were sitting in the back of Mr
Stephens' Super Snipe with pockets full of slugs
and .22 pellets. Mr Stephens had his mate Tosh in
the front and the boot brimmed with cedar-boxed
shotguns, a 303, a couple of .22 rifles and a slug
gun. We'd run the Fruit Fly Block at Wodonga
without a hitch. The Super Snipe is a smuggler's
dream, with hiding places everywhere. Mrs
Stephens' Esky was tucked safely under the back
seat.

It was a glorious day for killing, said Taillight.
Of course I'd have to be extra careful around the
guns, considering my current state of disgrace. A
shot through the heart would give little time for an
Act of Perfect Contrition.

We lurched off the tar and on to the dusty track that led to Barney Gehrig's winery, where Tosh had heard the local rabbits had beaten off the myxo and set up a paradise for their extended families. We'd packed half a dozen hessian bags in expectation. Not that Mr Stephens was your optimist. In fact he was a downright pessimist, as you might expect in an S.P. bookmaker. You'll make it up next time, he'd tell disappointed punters. Your turn next. One door closes, another door shuts was his punting philosophy. But he loved gunplay. He'd only shoot with his double-barrelled American-made Winchester shotgun, no matter if it was just a sparrow. The double whack would set him back on his heels but he was fearless against the rabbit. He loved his sport. Racing was his work but rabbits and birds were his life. And he was their death.

He wore thick wire eyeglasses with clip-on racing green aviator sunglasses when he was out and about. When he sighted his shotgun he pushed his glasses on to his forehead, under his hat, lined up his quarry and stuck his pipe out the other side of his mouth. Taillight said he slept in his hat with his pipe in his mouth. He hardly ever missed, and if he did he broke into a limping jig and let go a couple of fs and cs. Tosh was more interested in his bottled beer. He had demolished a couple by the time we pulled over near the huge Gehrig's Wines barn.

Barney Gehrig himself was this tall pencil-thin

wiry guy with skin that looked like it had been coloured in with an HB pencil. Waterstreets have been bottling his brown, white and tawny wines from wooden kegs into empty beer bottles for yonks. He looks a bit weatherbeaten because he planted his own grapes, picked them, squashed them, strained them and then delivered them in casks all by himself in an old Ford flat-top with his name on the driver's side. But Barney Gehrig's paddocks were home to millions of rabbits who must have loved the plonk and a few draught horses who pulled the wagon if the Ford played up.

Inside the wooden barn with its fading painted signs of vintages past, Barney kept two giant vats of fermenting wines. One white and the other tawny. I think his brown was a bit of both. Each vat had planks three times the size of railway sleepers going round in a circle, held together by huge iron rings. There was a homemade stepladder nailed to each vat. From the ground you couldn't see inside, but if you climbed the dozen or so steps you could see acres of wine sitting there just waiting for something to happen. And Taillight made it happen.

Taillight's brown eyes lit up like flares. Come up here, he beckoned from the top rung of the white wine vat, and while I was mounting the stepladder his shorts and T-shirt landed on my head. Although I couldn't see, the loud splash was the unmistakable sound of boy bellyflopping into a vat of fresh white wine. By the time I got to the top Taillight had done a lap to the other side and was squirting wine out of his mouth like a red-headed fountain. Don't swallow it, I cried.

Come on in, it's warm.

Even though it was Gehrig's finest white wine, it looked pretty dark and greenish – but I could tell he was naked. He never wore underwear. They didn't make his size, he often boasted, holding his crutch in his palm. I dipped my finger in. It was yukky. He splashed me and double dared me to get in. There was no use telling him about my confirmation vow never to touch liquor. Taillight was a public dog, and technically swimming in wine is not drinking it. Next thing, I was in my underdaks and holding my nose, plunging feet first into Barney Gehrig's September 1961 vintage fresh white wine. Naturally enough, Taillight triple dared we piss into it, which we did, and before long we were racing each other from side to side.

Mr Stephens was so angry he took his pipe out of his mouth before cursing us and threatening to take us straight home without a single shot. He knew how to get two boys out of a wine vat. We towelled down on a couple of the hessian bags from the boot.

Taillight set off into the paddocks with bare feet and his hair sitting up in red licks, a .22 in his hand. Tosh and Mr Stephens had a shotgun each. I had to make do with a slug gun. Lucky there's no tigers around Albury or I'd be in big trouble.

The Stephens family were natural sportsmen. Mr Stephens took bets on horses, greyhounds, trotters, pacers, the footy, all codes, even flies on walls I suspect. In fact, anything where there was a quid to be made. Every table in their house had green felt on it. Taillight had really introduced me to literature and the wonderful world of books. He gave me *The Sporting Globe* and *Miller's Race Guide* which had every major race result since the 1860s in every capital city in Australia, with all the place-getters, weights and jockeys. I lapped it up like water. I found out all sorts of things about the world, like all horses have the same birthday, 1 August, which means there must be a hell of a hootenanny between horses nine months before. Every horse in the whole world must do it on the same day. It makes the rest of the year a bit of a drag for them. Taillight and I congratulated each other on not being horses.

It was not only on the track that the Stephenses reigned supreme, but in the field they adopted the same scorched earth policy. If anything moved, two blasts of Mr Stephens' super shooter followed by a couple of .22 rounds from Taillight soon gave Barney Gehrig's paddocks a severe case of lead poisoning. The rabbits had little to fear from Tosh, whose first priority was to place his big beer bottle on the ground before he took aim. There was plenty of time to burrow down. Taillight was a rabbit's worst nightmare. A penny bunger down a rabbit hole caused them to run out of another hole, where the Stephenses waited with guns raised, and rabbit family life was in tatters. The ultimate weapon was a string of a hundred or so tom thumbs, which not only exploded in small blasts in the tunnels but jumped and jacked for yards underground, scaring the bejesus out of bunnies for miles. They bobbed up out of the ground all around, and there was furballs and rabbit meat on the blackboard for Mrs Westie's counter lunches for weeks after.

We dropped two hessian bags of rabbit parts in the hotel kitchen on the marble table and joined Mr Stephens and Tosh in the side bar for a post-battle squash. Mum was up and about for the first time in days, behind the bar, red lipstick making her look a little pale despite whirls of rouge and powder on her cheeks. My spirits always lifted to see her on her feet and out of bed. She was doing the Sunday night shift by herself; Dad was with some customers in the beer garden, encouraging the boozing. Not that they needed much. Dad's face beamed like a full moon when Mum was working. He welcomed the great white wine hunters when he saw Taillight and me walking rabbit-bloodstained but happy through the lounge door. Tosh had earlier let the cat out of the bag and Mr Stephens told the bar of our adventures. He spoke in the strangest way: his lips never seemed to move, his pipe slid from one side of his mouth to the other, coughs were like commas, hacks like full stops; but everybody nodded, laughed and understood his special sign language.

Before lights out, Dad was singing the latest hit, *Moon River*, and Tosh, who didn't have his finger on the pulse of Mid-States Radio Melody Bar's new records, joined in with *Ol' Man River*. No one seemed to notice. I was doing the puzzles from the comics in the Sunday papers. One of my favourites was joining the dots to reveal a stagecoach or giraffe or whatever. Mum was still on shandies, with Dad keeping an eye on her between songs. During *Galway Bay* I joined the freckles on Taillight's face with the black felt pen from behind the bar. It looked more like a spider web than anything else. Mrs Stephens would have needed all the methylated spirits in the house to scrub him up for school in the morning.

In Mum's good periods she tried to make up for the downtime. She rose at sparrow's fart and got us dressed and down for breakfast before Jimmy B had lit the stove. Early mornings in September were still brass monkey weather. You know, freeze the balls off a brass monkey. There's something really punishing about Catholic schools in Albury. St Thomas Aquinas had a winter uniform of Stamina grey wool suits with a free set of cards available from Mates's store's lower ground floor men and boys wear. What is it with the Catholic church and knees? None of the kneelers at St Pat's had any cushioning, unlike St Matthew's Methodist Church. At school we spent hours a day on our knees in the aisles next to our desks praying for forgiveness for sins we hadn't yet committed but would soon just to balance the books. Then to make matters worse our knees were left to the elements in the middle of winter. You'd expect the highest place in Heaven after all that. Blue goosebumps grew from my kneecaps and the thigh skin turned into old blotting paper with blue creeks of blood running every-where like an irrigation area. We weren't allowed to wear long pants but some of the boys would sneak into Rockman's Menswear to get measured up for them. They'd never buy them but Mr Jenkins loved running his yellow cloth tape measure around the boys' waists and nudging his knuckles into their crotches for the inside leg length. Some of the boys liked it as much as Mr Jenkins and tested their growth patterns nearly every week.

The strangest thing was happening during this last term in Albury. It's not something that I was very proud of. It was like I had no control over it, like some weird toxin had gotten into my system. An incredible and irresistible urge overcame me. I didn't fight it. It happened before I knew it. I was doing my homework. My good angel must have arm-wrestled my bad angel, and now although I still kept up the bad stuff like the rubbing and swearing and skylarking behind Brother Farrell's back while he wrote on the blackboard, whenever I got home or early in the morning before I caught the bus, I had *Poems of Spirit and Action* out, learning lines, or drawing geometric cones with a compass. Even in Latin, I was learning the verbs in all tenses including past, present and imperfect. Not only did I know what a meniscus was but I could spell it. I was turning into a consch like David Pugh, the only boy in class with glasses. You wouldn't want to get caught studying or reading up. On the bus I'd wrap a comic around the maths book. Luckily, no one ever suspected I was swotting. It must be sort of hereditary: Dad had his folded racing guide missal. Homework was so un-me. At St Thomas Aquinas, academic excellence was to be achieved only accidentally, except for Hayden Sir Sir Livermore. Any other way opened you up to ridicule. Mediocrity was your benchmark. We stretched towards the middle. Nothing else would do.

So now I had a hatful of secrets: the rubbing, the secret studies and the bedwetting. And of course Mum.

Twelve

In Albury before the spring of 1961, I had discovered the real hidden horror of childhood. Everything was what it seemed. If you scratched the surface on top, you got to the surface underneath. It was duco on duco with no undercoat. But now things were changing right before my eyes and under my nose. Everything was on the cusp of something else. The world was on the brink of the war to end all wars. The Health Department wanted to put poison in the people's drinking water. Menzies had brought the country to its knees and had almost unbelievably been kicked out of power. Mayor Bunton had been beaten in the polls and briefly ousted. Things I once believed in with all my heart, like transubstantiation and the Shroud of Turin, were beginning to seem like bad jokes. Papal bulls were turning into papal bullshit. My own voice was breaking, even if too slowly for my liking. I was on the cusp of childhood and boyhood. Next year I would be going to boarding school in Sydney, and already I missed the smell of Mrs Westie's days-old brewing brown tea at the back of her stove.

Not only was I growing up, but so was Albury itself. Canberra and Sydney were not Albury's mother and father and were not going to make Albury's mind up on fluoride. Cleaver Bunton said the people of Albury were old and wise enough to make their own minds up. All of us were coming of age. Traffic lights were just around the corner for Dean Street's busiest intersection. Ground was being broken near the old Thurgoona Road to build Albury Aerodrome with a mile-long tar runway, long enough to take a 44-passenger Fokker Friend-ship at full throttle.

Mum read the *Border* out loud. Mayor Bunton argued at a recent Council meeting that if we aldermen get a headache as a result of dealing with the fluoride question, would this be any grounds for lacing the city water supply with aspirin and forcing it upon the general public? Dad stubbed out one of his cigarettes into a saucer of butts and peered through the pall above the table-top. People were not going to have fluoride shoved down their throats. It's undemocratic. People should be able to choose, he said. It's what I would have fought for in the War if I didn't have to repeat the leaving, he added. It's unAustralian, Mum agreed.

The fluoride tide was turning at the Waterstreet family breakfast dining table. Soon enough, boarders from other tables were joining in the chorus for free choice and the rights of man. They sat up straight from the short chains holding their knives and forks. Captain Jack Saunders (retired) branded the pro-fluoride camp as cranks. J-J-Jack S-S-Shiebs was as angry as an ant and suggested a b-b-b-boyc-c-cott. Everyone was agreed. It's a matter of personal choice, declared Dad, it's our birthright whether or not to join in. I couldn't help myself. Don't forget to vote on Saturday, when it's compulsory, I said. Dad grimaced and grumbled smartarse out of the side of his mouth. Bill, language! But it was true. I was turning into a smartarse. Next I'll be using crossword puzzles for toilet paper. I was already too big for galoshes and now I was getting too big for my boots.

Dean Street looked like trench warfare had broken out between the shopkeepers on the Wodonga side and those on the North Albury side. The PMG were laying street-long trenches down either side, breaking up the tar and bitumen worse than the Bonegilla Army tanks on Anzac Day. Four-feet deep trenches lay the entire length of Dean Street, from the Terminus Hotel to the Globe Hotel. They were for the coaxial cables joining

Sydney and Melbourne together like a huge plastic umbilical cord. When it was done, all telephone, television and electrical messages could instantly travel between Sydney and Melbourne without worrying about fallen power lines in a thunderstorm or from lightning. It wouldn't be exactly instantly as Brother Farrell pointed out because nothing travels faster than the speed of light except his flying fingers of flung chalk. But it meant Albury could tap into the massive telecommunications advance and engage in three-way phone calls with Sydney and Melbourne. We lived in Lucky Town, New South Wales. Albury was tapped into the world – unless some careless farmer ploughed through the coaxial while planting. We were safe for a while, at least until the next Anzac Day. Television would still only be available to the lucky households of life's lottery winners with thirty-foot towers capable of reaching the GMV Channel 6 waves from Shepparton. It had taken them three months to dig up Dean Street, which is about a mile long. At this rate they should reach Sydney in the year 2535 and by then they would have invented colour television. Dad said those PMG workers wore out two shovels a day just leaning on them.

The coaxial was part of Menzies' plan to dig ourselves out of the recession. It hardly made up for the standard gauge debacle or the sky-high interest rates that drove all the bars mad every night. We were economising at home in many ways. There was a double bill at the Skyline Drive-In in Wodonga. *Mardi Grass* with groan Pat Boone but yeah *River's Edge* with Ray Milland. And the Movietone news. And a cartoon. Dad pulled over about half a mile from the Skyline entrance and put all the boys – me, John, Peter and the Hood – in the boot. Katherine Ann was allowed to stay in the front seat. We sailed straight through the sentry ticket box-office with three tickets please but had to wait until the news started before Dad could whistle his secret all clear and press the release button to let us climb out of each other's arms and legs and on to the blessed tarmac of the drive-in. We came as three and left as seven. Human loaves and fishes said Dad on the way home. Oh Bill, you're awful. Our strong sense of survival came from our history of being thrashed for centuries by the British in Ireland, then seeking sweeter soil in the South for the potato after the Great Famine, and building something out of the nothing by the Mighty Murray River. All my parents were Irish except for Mum and Dad.

But it wasn't all doom and gloom. Some people started to feel sorry for themselves when things got tough. If they started thinking that way then they were more inclined to have a beer or two to try and cheer themselves up. Inevitably, after a couple of cheering beers the full impact of their shocking personal and financial position seemed to become clearer and more impossible. Then they started to drink even more to drown their sorrows. Before long they were crying into their beers. Publicans got it coming and going.

Tommy Meehan was a full-time painter. Not your Green Indonesian Woman or Red Sails in the Sunset but a house painter. He was also a part-time country and western singer, and he sang on some special Friday nights at Waterstreets, changing out of his white and duck-egg paint splattered overalls in the gents toilet and into the latest Nashville shirt, all red and black with a line of green tassels hanging down across his back and along the sleeves. Times were tight, and when Tommy was short of a quid he would leave Dad with his guitar case containing his pride and joy Gibson acoustic guitar as a guarantee for the loan of a pound or two. Dad wrote it up in the black cash book under the bar which held Albury's secret financial position. Who owed what to Dad. You'd be surprised who got a little short and needed to be tided over until the next pension cheque. If anyone got behind, Dad got his friend Police Sergeant Townley to pay a friendly visit. Nothing rough, just a tap on the front door with the marked police car out the front of the house. This usually got Dad 80% of the debt and Townley pocketed the rest for the commission and overhead.

That and the Christmas whip-around of the hotel-keepers for a donation was one of the many perks for your Albury stationed cops. There was nothing wrong with law enforcement. It was the law that got it wrong. The cops just made it work.

So Tommy regularly handed his black guitar case over the counter to Dad and got a loan, which he usually paid out of his next pay cheque from the painting. However, Dad heard he was playing at the opposition pub one night. In the next block down Smollett Street, Brady's Railway Hotel was the one true enemy. We competed furiously for the favours of the fickle boozing punters. Waterstreets was a bloodhouse according to some. If you were barred from Brady's it was bad enough. But to be barred from Waterstreets was the end of the line. After that it was under the railway bridge or down by the riverbank.

Anyway, Dad was puzzled how Tommy could play at Brady's when he had put the guitar case in the back storeroom as security for a short-term loan. When we opened the guitar case it had two house bricks in it instead of the Gibson. Dad was furious. It didn't matter that Tommy always paid. It was the principle of the thing. Dad had been taken for a fool. But not for long. He never accepted house bricks from Tommy after that and Tommy never played at Brady's again. Dad said he sorted him out, whatever that meant. Dad was really a soft touch. In the big black cash book he gave credit where credit was often not due. He understood the pain of men hanging out for a port wine brandy with empty pockets and no prospects until pension day.

Heaven only knew, as Aunt Faith would say, why I was going to boarding school next year. My Aquinas uniform wasn't even one year old. We'd have to buy a whole new wardrobe in Sydney for Waverley College. It seemed like a real waste, with Menzies Bloody Credit Squeeze and Dad's licence hearing coming up. You couldn't tell your parents you didn't want to go, not with all the sacrifices they were making. Nana had sent Dad to boarding school during the War. Boarding schools in Sydney were much cheaper then because the rich were shipping their kids to the country in case the Japs bombed Sydney. Maybe Nana thought Albury might be a prime target for the Japs, with its beautiful natural wonders, primary and secondary industries, and the Weir.

Like I was saying before, I was beginning to notice that people didn't always say what they meant or meant what they said. Many times it was just the opposite. Aunt Faith would be scrubbing all the brass candlesticks from the church, dozens of them standing upright on her rosewood dining table, darning Father Bongiorno's robes or socks, preparing picnic lunches, getting ready to pick up one of the orphans from St John's Orphanage, snipping flowers out of her garden for a church function and saying to herself over and over again: no rest for the wicked, no rest for the wicked. Wicked! Jolly John XXIII should declare her a saint on the spot. With Aunt Faith, charity always began at home.

A special school assembly took place in the quadrangle before the first class of the day. After we packed our lunches into our desks and unpacked homework from our bags on to the teacher's table, each class gathered in groups standing around and gasbagging until Brother Quinlan blew his massive silver whistle, snapping each class into platoons of erect schoolboys. The Unchristian Brothers ruled by fear. Each one had a leather strap inside his black side pocket, ready to administer six of the best at the drop of one of their black hats. My Uncle Bob Carrol the bootmaker had not only been stitching new leather straps together for the Unchristian Brothers since corporal punishment was invented to repel sinning, but if the stitching frayed from overuse, he fixed them like new on his foot-pedalled sewing machine. It hurt even more, knowing that your own flesh and blood was helping arm the enemy. It was like being shot with your own gun.

This Monday morning assembly began with

morning prayers and a wrap-up of how the Aquinas footy teams had played over the weekend. I wasn't much for your team sports, being all arms and legs and as weak as a kitten. Mum said I was growing too fast. I thought it wasn't fast enough. Anyway, I got enough exercise with swimming in the wine, shooting rabbits and galahs and working behind the bar. There was time enough for sport later, when I would order one of the Bullworkers advertised in Dad's men's magazines hidden at the back of his sock drawer. Some of the natural athletes in my class carried spring wire chest expanders in their schoolbags and would pull them across their chest with the handles on either side at every opportunity. It was impossible for a boy who was growing too fast. If by some miracle I ever got the expander opened across my chest it immediately sprang back, catching my shirt and some skin before I dropped it screaming blue murder with red pinch marks around my nipples. Hayden Sir Sir Livermore could do it with an arm tied behind his back, standing on one leg. He was your all-rounder, best bowler, swimmer, runner, class captain and dux of First Year Gold. God answered all his prayers before he even asked. With Hayden Sir Sir Livermore the Lord giveth and giveth and giveth, and never taketh away.

After more prayers, we sang Hail Queen of Heaven, the Ocean Star, Guide of the Wanderer

Here Below. Brother Quinlan announced that there was to be a radio debate that morning on Radio 2AY right after the Chickabidees. All normal lessons starting at 11 a.m. were being suspended for the duration of the debate and each class could listen on their radios. Local businessmen had all chipped in to have each classroom installed with the latest multi-valved radio. There were problems earlier in the year because the radio reception in North Albury really tested the capacity of the 2AY transmitter on top of the two-storey Permewan Wright building in Town. It was fixed by having yards of red wire aerial running up to the corrugated iron roof which acted like a giant satellite dish.

The good news just kept on coming from Brother Quinlan. Next week we were to get a half-day off school for the Albury Show. It wasn't a Feast Day, so you didn't have to go to Mass. It was a real public holiday, confined only to the lucky citizens of Albury. Kids in Wodonga would have to go to school. That made it all the sweeter.

Brother Farrell read the roll call. Tibor Toth was absent. Even when he was there the name Tibor Toth was always followed by a titter around the class. It's just such a funny name. Tibor Toth. He had a big round head the size of a watermelon with bright white hair the colour of one of Katherine Ann's kewpie dolls. He used to wear galoshes, even in First Year at Aquinas. Galoshes were something you grew out of, like tricycles, but the Toths all wore galoshes whether it was wet or not. Grown-ups like me wore gumboots if it was pissing down. There's nothing better than landing smack bang in the middle of a puddle, straight off the bus, and splashing everyone else but leaving you high and dry in your gumboots. One of the perks of adolescence.

I sat next to Norbert Baczynski who looked like one of those German guys from the War on the run in South America you see in the papers from time to time. Except he was Polish. But like Aunt Faith says of anyone born overseas, especially anyone from the Bonegilla Migrant Camp, They're all New Australians. I'd like to go overseas but there's so many New Australians over there, she said. Norbert and I used to be great mates once, hoarding loads of black diamonds and precious stones we had found in the brick quarries at the back of Lavington in shoe boxes under our beds. Our friendship suddenly cooled for some reason when we found out the diamonds were worthless pieces of black rock. The partnership dissolved for lack of funding.

My cousin Tom Faith was still a great friend and I half-lived at his place, my home away from hotel, but we had gone in different directions. He followed the path of plastic aeroplanes, jigsaws, making his own bed, doing family stuff like picnics, writing AMDG on his homework and believing it helped, going to Mass when you didn't have to and not ducking out to Dean Street during the week to drink milkshakes at the Hume Weir Café and watch the black and white television in Mates's window. To be fair to him, he hadn't really met Taillight so there were excuses.

Another thing high school makes you notice is what I think is called class consciousness. But First Year Black never gave First Year Gold the respect it deserved. In fact it was quite the opposite. Black regarded themselves as the cocks of the walk, most of them were the best footy players and sportsboys. In fact a lot of those in Gold aspired to be in Black and ran dead in exams. The guys in Black seemed more fun. The pressure was a lot less. Geography was a breeze. On the Hume Highway of life, many of my class sought safety in the median strip. There weren't too many Taillights among them.

We were all excited about the debate. It would kill time and save us at least one lesson, maybe two. But the waiting for it seemed to drag so long that the time seemed to go in slow motion, minutes like hours, seconds like minutes, so that when you weighed up the balance, by lunchtime it was about square. Debating at Aquinas was an optional extra, like air-conditioning, and who wanted to do extra if it was optional? Debaters would have wonderful speaking voices, said Brother Farrell. What other sort of voices are there for God's sake? Public speaking was not for me. I debated once and dried up completely, blushed like a Red Indian and nearly wet myself in front of the entire class. Me, who otherwise is hardly ever at a loss for words. Nothing came out. I think I'm more your Public Bar speaker, your one on one, not up in front of the whole class.

Hayden Sir Sir Livermore led Aquinas First Year Gold Debating Team. He spoke like he'd swallowed a dictionary. He used a lot of what Taillight called four-cylinder words. First Year Black decided their debates with fists. Brother Farrell admonished us to listen carefully to the great fluoride debate and we might learn a thing or two about public speaking and the art of debating. He fiddled with the radio dial trying to find 2AY. It sounded like a shortwave radio in one of those World War Two movies, whooping up and down until the unmistakable golden voice of Mayor Bunton came through the speaker like velvet. One of Nature's Gentlemen, murmured Brother Farrell.

Bunton the Great Moderator with the grandest voice that God ever breathed breath into announced that he was not participating in the debate. The City Council had long decided to leave it to the people to make up their minds what to do with their bodies. He personally was not against the fluoride but he was most definitely opposed to forcing people who did not want fluoride in their water for any reason to have it put in. People ought to be well-informed in a great democracy like ours and what better way, he said, than by the magic of radio which would enter the lounge rooms of families, the workplaces, the farmhouses, the shops of this great city. And shithouses, someone whispered behind me. Shh, said Brother Farrell with his long chalky finger to his lips, cocking a huge hand-cupped ear to the Bakelite and his face frowning like a hidden magnet does iron filings on paper.

In the luxuriously appointed 2AY sound studio were key representatives of the two sides, for and against. Dr Hogan led for the fors. The man from Queensland, Mr Harding, who had travelled hundreds of miles from Rockhampton, opened for the against. Mayor Bunton described the atmosphere in the studio as electric, with all the speakers gathered around the mike and as many as sixteen interested members of the public in the studio auditorium. But before I introduce our auspicious speakers, he said, a word from our generous and wonderful sponsors, Show Drive Baker's Motor Car Yard. [Mayor Bunton in a posh voice.] We must reach our show sales drive quota. We'll show you a deal you can't refuse on any Austin or Morris. See us now or see us at the Show. See our magnificent range of cars and then try us on trade-in price. Morris A50 £772. Morris Minor £873. Morris Major £997.10s. Morris Oxford £1160. Wolseley 15/60 £1297.10s. Austin

A40 £925. Lancer Deluxe £1030. A/60 £1200. All available at Show Drive Baker Motors, opposite Hoyts in Olive Street Albury. Phone number 629.

It was a piece of advertising genius. From left field, Baker Motors slipped in the English cars between Ford and Holden at the start of the greatest debate the Murray Valley had ever heard. And read by Mayor Bunton himself, live. Those Morrises will be walking out of the showroom.

Dr Hogan opened boldly, saying fluoridation was the greatest preventive health measure of the twentieth century. He was a family man with children of his own, whose welfare he held close to his heart, which you could almost hear beating under the pat of his hand on his chest. He had been associated with inspections of the dental health of school children of Albury and was astounded by what he found. On average there were 10 teeth missing, decayed or filled in each mouth at the age of 9 and 15 of the same in children at the age of 14. Everyone in class smiled at this, conclusively proving his observations grossly underestimated. There were hardly enough good teeth in the whole class to make one decent set between us. Excepting, of course, Hayden Sir Sir Livermore, whose brilliantine smile almost caused you to squint. Dr Hogan implored the listening audience to leave our children, born and unborn, a legacy. Jesus Mary and Joseph. What other type of audience is there for a radio show than a listening audience? Tee hee, we giggled. Shh, went Brother Farrell.

Mr Harding banged on and on about Christian freedom and the right to choose what goes into our bodies. The next speaker, Mrs Betty Guyner, was better and deadly. Surely as a mother I should be rather guided in health matters by these immensely trained men than by the arguments of a professional antagonist imported at someone's expense from another State. Are you, Mr Harding, interested in the welfare of Albury's children? I doubt it. She really had stuck it up the man from Rockhampton.

From time to time Mayor Bunton had to throw his majesterial weight around to break up cat fights that developed. For every doctor's report one side had there was one on the other. Dr Hogan described one of the opposing speakers as a blow-in from Queensland and the other as a railwayman. It was strong language indeed. Railwayman. Dr Hogan was told to look in the mirror and he might see Charlie Chaplin in *The Great Dictator*. Mr Roach, against fluoride, rattled off the names of towns in the USA which had rejected fluoride. This is not some hillbilly town in Tennessee, countered Dr Hogan.

Anyway, the whole thing went on for ages before Mayor Bunton called a halt to proceedings and left it to the people to decide. He finished up with a commercial for Preston Motors and Holdens.

He was very even-handed in everything. Time went so quickly that it was lunch before we knew it. Brother Farrell did a mini version of the Angelus and let us out to eat. There was an especially long queue at the tuck shop waiting to order lollies.

Brother Plunkett introduced us to the incredible world of the slide rule. Fractions were now instantly available at your fingertips. The slide rule is what distinguishes man from the lower animals. You could solve any of the world's problems with one of these things. It was just a piece of white plastic with another piece of clear plastic that went up and down. There were minute black and red coloured measurements on both pieces. Of course, Sir Sir Livermore and Sir Sir Pugh already had them. While the rest of us were doing long division on paper with figures and lines descending the page like staircases, they were whisking the slide rule to and fro and putting up their hands. Sir, Sir. I wasn't convinced the slide rule was the answer. There was a sense of satisfaction to long division on the page that sort of rounded things off. The slide rule was a cheat. But Brother Plunkett declared the slide rule was the way of the future so I determined I must have one.

Brother Farrell took us for the last period of the day. He was a big fan of the English language but Esler caught him a beauty. Greg Esler had lucked into Gold, maybe because Black was full, but he knew a thing or two about a thing or two. When Brother Farrell asked if anyone knew the meaning of condescending, Esler quick as a flash put his hand up. Sir, Sir. You could tell Brother Farrell was pleasantly surprised and said Yes, Esler. It's a Greek parachutist, Sir. We all nearly pissed ourselves. I had to hold my nose real tight until tears came. Brother Farrell to his credit didn't give Esler the strap. After we all settled down and wiped our noses with our sleeves he clipped him hard on the back of the head, but in the sort of way a nice bully punches you in the soft part of your arm, kind of saying in a way you old bastard. Esler looked relieved after the cuff and he was envied all the way home on the bus. I think Aunt Faith got that one wrong. Everyone likes a smart alec.

One of the worst by-products of Menzies Bloody Credit Squeeze was that Dad had to let one of the barmen go and do double shifts himself. He didn't seem to mind but I did because he was harder to get chips and squashes off than the bar usefuls. Bar uselesses he called them. Your father works his fingers to the bone, said Mum. I must have heard that a million times. It was like some family litany. Your father works his fingers to the bone. Your father is. Rushed off his feet. Your father does. The work of ten men. Your father never stops. Your father. Who aren't in Heaven.

There was no use asking Dad for chips, spoil your dinner and all that, but I got a middie of squash which was sorely needed after absorbing all there was to know about the slide rule. Chips were available later from the pigeonhole at the back of the bar near the stock fridge if Dad was distracted up the other end and I could poke myself through the pigeonhole and hook a packet off the chrome shelf with the tips of my inky fingers.

Meanwhile in the front bar Jack Davies and his mate Uncle were bending their arms on one of the great boozing benders they went on from time to time. Jack Davies was a tall elegant man who always wore clean, ironed white shirts and dapper store-bought suits whether he was completely para-lytic or not. He ran his bird-boned fingers through smokey white-grey hair when it flopped over his forehead. At the hairline his hair was the colour of tobacco stains. He always wore a neatly Windsor-knotted tie with the coat of arms of some organisa-tion whose history he could and often did talk about for hours. Even if no one but Uncle was there, who was deaf as a doorpost. But I guess that wasn't the point. Jack Davies' hands were a gold-mine. Uncle was there to stand guard over them during week-long booze-ups, to ensure no harm came to the source of their endless bingeing. Jack wasn't your usual alcoholic customer, putting the word on everyone for a drink. He was swimming in the money. He was a dental technician who made the dentures for real dentists. Dentists were trained to pull teeth, fill teeth and straighten teeth, but only the dental technician could make them and Jack, even on his bad days, made a mean set of enamel teeth. Technicians were supposed to work only through dentists but people started going to Jack directly, cutting out the middle man, and getting a new set of upper and lowers for £10. Registered dentists charged £25 for the same set.

He worked from a garage cum laboratory up in East Albury. Uncle was like his hunchback helper. Jack really fell on his feet when he got the Australian Army contract. There were hundreds of vacancies in the heads of volunteers and Jack loved his work. There was more lead in Australian soldiers' mouths than the Japs ever shot into the rest of their bodies. And when the lead fell out, Jack's work began. He measured them out in gooey Plasticine at the Bonegilla Army Camp by the dozen, churned out shoe-boxes of dentures by the end of the week and then he started all over again. Seven days a week. For months on end. Then he and Uncle would hit the local pubs, one by one, starting with the toffy New Albury in Kiewa Street and finishing up days later at Waterstreets.

Jack pulled big notes one at a time from a wet wad the size of a football which he kept inside his coat pocket. Uncle helped them on their way to the till. No one knew whether Jack and Uncle were related or not. Jack ordered two beers and two double Scotches for himself and Uncle. Benders could last for days or weeks, according to the vapours. The army would have to make do, leaving soldiers mashing their food, because Jack was one of the best.

Drunks from miles around loved Jack's benders. He always shouted the bar wherever he went, and drunks followed him and Uncle from pub to pub down Dean Street like it was Anzac Day every day for alcoholics. He was the Pied Piper of the pissed. He held court in the Public Bar with Ernie Carpenter eyeing his lovely long white hands. Everyone laughed lots at his jokes. Especially Uncle. Uncle could lip read when Jack was sober but couldn't understand a thing when Jack was drinking, but that didn't seem to matter really. You had to be a publican like Dad to speak fluent drunk.

Now that Mum was on her feet, she nearly always went shopping late in the afternoon. I quietly plotted a detour into the stationery department of Blakes Busy Book Bazaar. One of the great things about going shopping with Mum was afternoon tea at the Gala Lounge. Mum packed her shopping bags into the rich red vinyl cubicle against the far wall and we slid on our bums into the middle so both of us could look out on to the passing parade along Dean Street. The Gala was smack bang in the middle of Albury's busiest thoroughfare, intersecting Dean Street and the T & G Lane. Pedestrians from all walks of life passed. Sheep farmers in Baxter boots and wide brown felt hats, cow cockies in their town clothes of moleskins and tweed sports jackets, pregnant mothers to be in their husbands' shirts, solicitors looking for clients, clients avoiding creditors, accountants with heads full of numbers and shirt pockets full of pens, high school boys on the prowl, indifferent tunicked schoolgirls doing everything but avoiding eye contact, people looking for other people.

Mum sipped on Lipton's Finest Ceylon Tea with her little finger half-cocked while I sucked a chocolate malted milkshake through two straws. You couldn't get it into yourself quick enough. Mum ordered toasted bacon sandwiches for both of us. God I loved the home cooking at the Gala. Mrs Westie's wasn't home cooking. It wasn't even hotel cooking.

It was worth waiting in Ruby Dihood's ladies lingerie shop while Mum picked up pink panties and slips with her fingers from the glass-topped serving counter without any intention of buying. Shopping was an exercise, like golf. Just a way of having a good walk. To be fair, Mum loved to buy clothes for Katherine Ann. What I didn't like was her holding dresses against me, guessing Katherine Ann's height relative to mine. At Cann's Clothes the salesgirls put the cash into the hollow of little wooden capsules which they screwed into a trellis of wires going across the ceiling. Then they pulled a rope handle like a toilet chain and the capsule shot across the room to a central cash place where it was emptied and sent screaming back with a handwritten receipt and change.

Blakes Busy Book Bazaar had round slide rules. The salesman said they were even more accurate than the straight ones. But a circle wasn't a rule. He's off to Sydney next year, Mum told the salesman, who raised his eyebrows so high that his eyeglasses fell from the top of his head on to the tip of his nose. Well, he'll need the best to keep up with those city boys. Where's he going? Cranbrook, Scots . . .? Waverley College. Oh. I haven't heard of that. He wrapped a straight slide rule in brown paper with a lot of sticky tape. On the way home we stopped at every shopfront, and then some. I didn't mind. It was great to have Mum vertical again.

But I couldn't wait to run upstairs and tear the paper off the slide rule. What was happening to me? I was turning into a swot.

Thirteen potato

What really put our town on the map was the Albury Spring Show. Show Day was a school holiday across the board. Mayor Bunton cut the working day in half with a flourish of his Mont Blanc fountain pen, donated by a group of grateful constituents, declaring that it would have been a whole day for the working man but for the [Menzies Bloody] Credit Squeeze. Show Day brought the world to Albury and Albury to the world. It was bigger than *Ben Hur*, and Regent Picture Theatregoers knew what that meant. Albury became, for three days, the crossroads of the world.

There was something for everyone, mums, dads, boys, girls and even Taillight, who loved the Wheel of Death. Motorcycle riders in pitch black leather suits and wearing what looked like diving helmets rode their Harley Davidsons around and around a built-in-an-afternoon wooden circular coliseum until they were parallel to the ground while spectators watched from above. Taillight himself was born to drive in constant circles. The announcer called them daredevils. I called them mad.

Spring meant rain and every Show as far back as I can remember had a carpet of wet mud that caked on your socks and had to be peeled off when you got home. Mum took all of us this year, but I could wander off with Taillight while she took Katherine Ann, John, Peter and the Hood through the cream of district exhibits housed in the Great Albury Exhibition Hall. A wealth of local pride was laid out in a motif of grain samples, hops, tobacco, wines, preserves and the smaller district industries. A huge stall of different fruits made a map of Albury and district. A row of red apples like a graph line almost passed for the Mighty Murray River. By the end of the Show the bananas and peaches ponged the Exhibition Hall completely out and thousands of fruit flies illegally crossed the border for the decaying bonanza. Lines of showgoers waited to see the wool and textile exhibition but the smell of damp dags made me want to throw up.

The commerce stuff was strictly for the birds. Taillight and I were more at home up Sideshow Alley. Never mind the thousands of flowers in the horticultural section poking out of hundreds of neat rows of bottles. Never mind the arts and crafts, with hand-knitted jumpers with the Monument Hill on the front and Albury Railway Station on the back. Never mind the smell of cooking vats of produce, jam jars of stewing fruits, the endless rows of Fowler's Vacolas, the fat lamb carcass competition, the photographic show that was expected to reach new heights of quality this year. We cashed in a ten pound note for coins which filled our pockets like saddlebags. Mum put her slingback foot firmly down about going on the Ferris Wheel herself. Taillight and I had to take the kids up. They screamed blue murder when we rocked the carriage from side to side at the top. Mum didn't ask us to help much after that and we were free to explore the painted canvas tents by ourselves. Every couple of steps we stopped with our hands in our pockets and wiggled our bums so we would hear the tinkle of coins and feel them wobbly in our hands. God it was good to be loaded.

There's no use buying your sample bags early because you have to carry them around all after-noon. But we lined our stomachs with fairy floss and toffee apples. Taillight left a tooth in the sticky red coating after a bite. I tried to explain to him about the Tooth Fairy, that there wasn't really one I know but you could still play the game and get cash for it overnight by leaving it in a glass of water near your bed. He brushed the idea off with the tooth itself, which was lost in the deep of the mud.

People had come from as far afield as Wanga- ratta and Holbrook for the Show and we had to duck under arms and sample bags to get to the front of every marquee. Taillight wasn't keen to go in the Mirror Maze but I twisted his arm, which was just as well as I got lost somewhere inside and he got us both out by getting on his knees and looking under the mirrors for the exit. I wore two Mirror Maze Medals with pride, Taillight's and mine, both pinned to my top pocket for days.

Jimmy Sharman's Travelling Boxing Show troupe promised a round or two for a pound or two. Drunk farmers' sons were soon laid out flat by the little Thursday Islander on the drum. Sometimes you knew that the challenger from the crowd was part of the troupe. He was staying with the other fighters at Waterstreets. But they still put on such a good show that you couldn't care it wasn't the real thing.

The Dance of the Seven Veils by Sheila the Peeler and Vanessa the Undresser originally wasn't all that high on my list but Taillight ended up talking me into three shows, one after the other. Each performance finished with the last veils being stripped off with a flick by the red-coated ringmas- ter, exposing Sheila and Vanessa's blue-veined breasts to Taillight and me in the front row. He said, with a wink, don't tell your mothers. It was funny the first time but after three times it got a bit boring. Taillight's tongue hung out so far he almost tripped over it. He didn't say anything at all during the three shows but just moved his legs quickly like he wanted to go to the toilet, which he did shortly after the third show. He was much calmer thereafter.

I was fascinated by dwarves, tattooed men and ladies, monster boys, two-headed lambs – even if dead in big glass bottles – bearded women and that sort of stuff. Freak shows made me feel better about myself, my thin arms and legs, my sticky-out ears and turned up nose. I guess that's why I had such a soft spot for Vic the jockey. I ribbed Taillight that he could always get a job as Freckle Face. He punched me hard on the arm twice. It was numb until I got home, where knuckled bruises blew up like sergeant's stripes near my shoulder.

Mum and the kids were in the Ladies Lounge with sample bags, plastic rubber-banded windmills on wooden sticks, toffee apples and wide open eyes. Mum was off her feet, which were on one of the mottled red Formica tables. A flat shandy sat untouched near them. She was looking at it. Dad came in from the kitchen whistling aloud. What's this then? He grabbed the Hood in two huge hands and lifted him over his head and nearly into the ventilating propellers that hung from the ceiling. Oops! Mum was up in a flash and it was Bill, Bill, stop that, you nearly cut his head off. The Hood was too tired to care. We all were. Kids today, said Dad. When we were kids we were about your age.

Mum drank the shandy in one go.

Showtime meant a full house of Show people. The back yard burst with their cars, trucks and caravans. Year after year the Showies went from town to town across Australia, pitching their tents, staying at the same pubs and spending everything they made during the day that very night. They loved to party, Albury was party town, and Waterstreets was a party pub. They'd bunk two or three to a room to save costs. Dad didn't mind because he got it coming and going. What they didn't spend at the back of the house, we got at the front. The regulars and boarders loved the Showies and the back bar bulged at the sides after closing time. The front lights were dimmed after ten to keep up appearances and doors locked, except out the back. The Showies were bona fide travellers, of sorts, but nobody cared about the fine legal lines the first night of the Spring Show.

The identical Jackson twins came every year. You couldn't tell one from the other. They spoke the same, dressed the same, looked the same, but they loathed each other. We had to put them in rooms at the opposite ends of the hotel. They hated the sight of each other which was pretty strange considering how they looked. After the day's performance was over they wouldn't have anything to do with each other until the next day. In the back bar other Showies kept them well apart.

I snuck down for a squizz at things. A boy couldn't sleep with all the racket. Well, not this boy. The bearded lady was dressed like a man, knocking back schooners of brown bubbly beer and brushing the froth off her moustache. Mum and Dad and Big Jeff Eames were all working behind the bar, back and forth to the taps, and upending liquor bottles into shot glasses for those who needed supplementary assistance. The men who worked the merry-go-rounds were toasting the midnight shift of shunters who'd ducked down from the railway to relieve the pressure of the work. Every so often Dad would cough loudly and request quiet, which worked for a while but the grumbling and rumbling grew and grew until he had to cough again. A passing wowser could ring the police and there was no room in the back bar for any more drinkers.

Mum had a stool up the confessional end of the bar where a hole in the wall allowed orders to be taken for the Ladies Lounge. She had graduated from shandies to something stronger and beamed at me when I appeared like Foo at the confessional, moon face rising over two hands grasping the bar. A lemonade was just too easy. Mum in this mood was a pushover. Dad was too busy. Big Jeff Eames' glasses had fogged up, as indeed had he. Dad said Big Jeff served beer on the principle of one for the customer and one for himself. He drank all our profits. He could keep it up but the Showies were slowing him down. Dad put up with it on the grounds that help was hard to get and Big Jeff spilt more than he drank anyway these days.

The travellers brought their songs and stories with them and it wasn't long before they unpacked them. Floods and bushfires never stopped them getting to any town in the country, no matter how small. But Menzies Bloody Credit Squeeze was hurting everyone, especially the smaller towns. They regarded Albury as a big town. So did I. Didn't everyone? Of course the boxers from Sharman's brought their work home and fights broke out in flutters of activity but soon died down when Dad walked amongst them. If he ever needed a hand I was there. Luckily he could handle himself. I really couldn't fight my way out of a paper bag, unless it was wet.

All the shunters and locals bought crème de menthe after crème de menthe for Sheila and Vanessa. They shared room 22 which had a double bed. Their room number was a state secret, otherwise everyone would be up there trying to take a peek. Funny thing was I already had, thrice, that very afternoon, for a shilling a time with Taillight. They wore bright red lipstick and held each other's hands. Albury's night shift scared them a little. Unlike the Jacksons, they at least had each other. When the Jacksons were together they looked like reflections in the Mirror Maze, but the Dancers of the Seven Veils had little in common physically except their womanliness. They had breasts like the gun turrets on the Bismarck. Jack Davies and Uncle topped themselves and the girls up with drinks and dreams of double dating.

Mum plonked down on the stool and I ducked through the side office and into the bar and started serving beers. Although I was in my pyjamas I had Dad's Onkaparinga dressing gown on which trailed like a priest's robes behind me. Jimmy B, Captain Jack Saunders (retired), J-J-Jack S-S-Shiebs and the whole gang were shoulder to shoulder with the Showies in the Saloon Bar. Ernie Carpenter with his twin hooks for hands had found that there could be life after shunting and surgery. He fitted in with the Showies like a glove. The only way to keep things quiet was for Dad to recite by heart one of the great poems. Mum reckoned it was good for business because it drove them to drink. Dad patted the air and big Jeff shushed up and down the bar with his gigantic finger across his lips. Out of the smoke Dad's voice boomed:

There was movement at the station, for the
    word had passed around
That the colt from old Regret had got away
And had joined the wild bush horses – he was
    worth a thousand pound,
So all the cracks had gathered to the fray

and on and on. Poetry in Waterstreets back bar was a very different kettle of fish from Brother Quinlan's English class. There was a real music in the words. Everyone was quiet until Dad was done. He knew them off by heart. Some of the Showies had favourites of their own and being in show business they knew how to pull it off a treat. There was more poetry in the Saloon Bar that night than in the whole of *Poems of Spirit and Action*.

Every year an old woman called Ursula, must have been about forty, came to stay and set up a little tent with just two chairs and a table at the Showground right by the entrance. She was a fortune teller. Dad would always say she must work at the bank. She read palms, a crystal ball that resembled a giant marble, and teacups for money. By the look on her face nothing good was ever going to happen. Heaven knows what she saw ahead. Her mouth was an upside down grin. Hardly anyone spoke to her. She drank McWilliams sweet sherry in seven-ounce glasses and usually kept herself to herself.

During an interruption of silence between songs I asked her to tell me my fortune. She held my hand and glared at it. I thought maybe I was too young and lines had not yet developed. She cupped my hand and folded it in hers, causing creases to break out. Very interesting, she said. I was hooked. What? You will suffer great loss but great happiness. Get out of it, I replied. Never mind that, how will I do in the exams? She almost closed her eyes but continued to examine my hand somehow, turning it toward the dull light above the till. You will soon be leaving this place and going to the sea. You will be leaving your family behind. I had no idea what she was talking about. It was gobbledegook.

She was starting to give me the creeps, so I pulled my hand softly back. She looked straight at me and through me with her half-hooded eyes. So I said something smart like well the future's ahead of me is it? I topped up her sherry for free. I bet there's someone's palms you can't read, I quipped. She bet me another sherry and we shook on it. I beckoned Ernie Carpenter over and he made his way through the crowd using his shoulders. Ernie stood in front of her and lifted his two hooks waist-high. I won the bet hands down. Ernie went back to his seat but I really felt sorry for Ursula so I told her that it wasn't a real bet. She finally smiled. It turned out she was a regular person, suffering life's usual ups and downs. In fact she didn't pay for another drink all night, even though I'd won. There's no future in fortune telling, she said. The bottom fell out of reading tea leaves with the introduction of the tea bag. It's a wonder you didn't see it coming, I said.

They were still singing when I went to bed and suddenly remembered that I was going to boarding school next year. In Sydney. Near the Specific Ocean. Ursula couldn't have known that. If only she would concentrate on the Melbourne Cup winner. We could get the *Sporting Globe* before the races were run and Mum and Dad could really clean up and put Menzies Bloody Credit Squeeze and the straight-through gauge behind us forever. All the lemonade I drank downstairs made not wetting the bed almost impossible.

Fourteen potato

The Showies must have had mixed regrets that Luther the World's Strongest Man had not joined this year's Albury Spring Show but had decided to settle down in a fern nursery with a trapeze artist in Sydney. Luther could have carried their sick and aching bodies from the beds to the trucks, hooked up the trailers, winched up the Octopus, and beat them senseless to remind them not to drink before workdays.

In the dining room it wasn't exactly your Breakfast with the Stars. There were little upward licks of green stains at the mouth corners left uncovered despite lashings of red lipstick on the faces of the Dancers of the Seven Veils. The Showies were one of the highlights of the culinary year for Mrs Westie, a chance to showcase her talents. She had

prepared trays of pork sausages, eggs, fried toma-
toes and burnt bacon rashers. Most of the Showies
were no shows. The few who braved the breakfast
table turned their faces away from anything resembling food, as Mrs Westie's cooking sometimes did.
Mrs Westie mumbled It's a crying shame, it's a
crying shame, and tut-tutted about the evils of the
front of house. I couldn't see any onions on the
trays but she had the beginnings of tears gathering
in the corners of her eyes.

Mum and Dad had breakfast in bed. Dad split
the *Border Morning Mail* into two for them. He got
the headlines, sports, race results and comics. Mum
got Coles and Woolies specials and the Gymkhana
Roundup. He was as even-handed as Mayor Bunton, but in his own way. She wasn't really up to
reading. Last night boded badly. She put on a brave
and fighting face from the space between the pillows. Give us a kiss will you Charles. When she was
well and confident I was Charlie. I leant over and
kissed her before heading off to school. She put her
hand on the back of my head and held it hard
against her. Her hair smelt of cigarettes and her
breath of brandy. She held me tight until I burst
away with a Bye, Dad, bye, Mum. See ya.

In a way I saw Mum as a kind of Showie
herself. She stayed with us as long as she could,
until she got too sick, too run down, until the nerves
got too much, and then she travelled to different

places, pitched a tent and tried to get well. She'd return full of beans and medication, and we'd start all over again. When she was really bad at home there was a kind of invisible hospital curtain around her bed, with the kangaroo-skin doona over her body. None of the family would talk about it. It was a kind of fixture in the family furniture. When she was well she ruled with the sharp end of a feather duster.

As the years went by her trips to hospitals got further and further away from Albury. There wasn't much the local doctors could do for nerves, whatever they were. When Mum told me about shock treatment I thought she was having a lend. Later, when Dad confirmed it, my own hair stood on end. There were two ways to deal with the thought of Mum's pain. Either I obsessed about it endlessly or I forgot entirely. Strangely enough, it wasn't something I decided, it just happened. My head turned it off, like the radio, not even a red glowing valve at the back of my mind.

On the other hand, Dad had nerves of stainless steel. Punting disasters were shrugged off, police raids were like unofficial atomic bomb survival exercises, fights in the bar were sheer sports, Menzies Bloody Credit Squeeze and the standard gauge a government's madness and were treated the way farmers treated droughts and bushfires: part of Mother Nature's mysterious ways. There'd be good years around the corner. The singing never stopped. Only the songs and some of the singers changed.

One of the Wall of Death bikers gave me a lift to school on the back of his Harley. I was in Seventh Heaven. If I hadn't Brylcreemed my hair it would have swept back like Charlton Heston's did when parting the Red Sea. I clutched Mr Wall of Death as if my life depended on it. All I really wanted was for everyone I knew in the whole wide world to see me, Aquinas tie trailing, school bag between me and Mr Wall of Death, and me leaning the wrong way at every turn to keep the bloody bike from falling. Taillight would have been red and bottle green with envy. The best part of stuff is the sharing. There's no use taking small steps in the dark by yourself. Except for the clothes closet of course. But by the time I got to school all I cared about was getting off and being alive. To my mind the bus is mightier than the bike from now on.

Frauenfelder and Purtle saw me disembike. Aquinas was on the block next to the Showground and Mr Wall of Death made the Harley stand upright and went to work, where he did much the same thing. Celebrity is a shallow and fleeting thing. One minute Frauenfelder and Purtle were quizzing me about every detail of the ride and the next minute they were off playing cricket with a tennis ball and half a fence plank without me. I was left standing singlehandedly pulling my skidmarked underpants out of my bum-crack with shaking fingers.

All day the air inside the classroom vibrated with merry-go-round music played on 33⅓ records, which often caught in a groove and repeated Teddy bears come out to play, to play, to play, to play until they were bumped by an irritated and hungover attendant. Loudspeakers promised kewpie dolls if you knocked down three cans with one ball; laughing twisting clowns with ping-pong balls; pea-shooters; merino sheep sales; dressage competitions; and best of all Sheila and Vanessa, the Dancers of the Seven Veils. Brother Farrell shouted his lessons. Nearly everyone answered his questions with a What? What was that Sir? God gave us two ears. One for Brother Farrell and one for the Show. It cut the learning right in half. The Wall of Death made Latin impossible. For the next two days, Aquinas boys were at school in body but most were being slung every which way by the Octopus and crunching down on toffee apples in spirit next door at the Showground. I daydreamed of watching the Dancers of the Seven Veils in Mum's three-dimensional swivelling make-up mirror.

The children of life's lottery winners would go to the show after school with extra play money, in the folding stuff not coins. The battlers skipped lunch or the bus and used the savings to get in. Taillight had sawn a hole in the fence at the back of the

Showground. As if that wasn't bad enough, he sold kids entry for half price. At this rate Taillight was bound to be one of life's lottery winners himself one day.

On the day the Showies took to the road in the form of the Hume Highway to Wagga Wagga, Ursula told me she wouldn't see me again. What, aren't you coming back, I asked. No, *you* aren't. Of course, silly me. She was right as usual. Next year I'd be at school in Sydney during the Spring Show. Ursula had the gift, no doubt about it. I made a point of saying goodbye to as many of the Showies as I could. They were in a rush because they had to pitch the Wagga Wagga Spring Show before that night's gala opening. It was bone-breaking work and from time to time one of the acts stayed on in a town, unable to continue to the next. Apparently it's not uncommon to run away from the circus.

When Mum was real sick, Dad would come downstairs for breakfast. He wasn't big on conversation first thing in the morning. He was still hoarse from reciting and singing all night, but a couple of Viscounts soothed his sore throat a treat. He read the *Border Morning Mail* from cover to cover, but back to front. He'd start from the sports pages and work his way through world events to current Albury affairs. Letters to the Editor were flooding into the *Border*, some so controversial they were anonymous. Dad handed me each page after he finished, so information-wise I was really only minutes behind him. It's funny how there's just enough news every day to fill a newspaper the next day. No more. No less. On dull days there should be blank pages in the *Border*. There never is.

It was all in there. Plots in Kuwait, car racing safety inquiries, hepatitis epidemic in Corowa, and another story from Corowa about an ill woman using her curtains to signal for help. It was all happening in Corowa. Blackies Pharmacy had the new Phillips all-in-the-ear instrument that made all the other hearing aids old-fashioned. No ear buttons, no cords. Holbrook bowlers need run to the clubhouse no longer for shade – shade specially designed for their greens was now being erected. New brochures were available for New Australians at naturalisation ceremonies. Mayor Bunton would preside and the brochure – *This is Yours* – described in words and pictures the significance of the Queen, Parliament and the national heritage that naturalised citizens would assume. Else Hunz of Wise Street and Erwin Hunz of David Street were among many destined to fully join us as God's own in God's own. There was an offensive odour in Wodonga water. Mr Nugent, a local teacher described it as something similar to that of a dead beast. Drains in Leonard Street had become unbearable. The new Governor-General, Lord de

L'Isle, made his first visit to Melbourne. The Wodonga-Tallangatta passenger rail service was closed for lack of support. Adolf Eichmann made a million-word statement after interrogation by Israeli police, made up of 3700 pages weighing about 11 lbs. Israeli police had a way of not only making you talk but making you never shut up. A half dozen bottles of beer wouldn't have got Eichmann very far in Israel. From among his million words the *Border* quoted:

> There was screaming and shrieking. I was too excited to look at the van. Later I followed the van and saw the most horrifying sight I ever saw in my life. The corpses were thrown into a ditch as if they were animals – then their teeth were extracted.

Russia's second space man, Major Titov, was cheered by a gay Moscow, embracing his wife and getting kisses from a group of pretty girls. Communists were strange people, or their wives extremely tolerant.

The *Border* was the eyes and ears of the world outside Albury. It was the mouthpiece of Albury opinion at home, especially about the red hot issue of the next weekend. The people's referendum on fluoridation. The City Council had scrutinised and finally sanctioned the wording of the fluoridation questionnaire ballot paper. After much toing and froing, Mayor Bunton got his way. The question read: Are you in favour of fluoridation of Albury's water supply? You had to put the numbers 1 or 2 in the boxes noted as Yes or No. It seemed a pretty complicated method. But Mayor Bunton denied dissenting aldermen's protests of its obtuseness. It was clear, he said, and any mistaken ballot papers with missing numbers or ticks or unfilled boxes would be counted as No. It's little wonder he was mayor for life.

The whole question of the wording of the voting card arose when Mrs Redmond of Lavington claimed the fluoridation of water supplies would be detrimental to the health of her stud dairy cows. They were valued at from £200 to £300 each. Mayor Bunton solemnly read the letter to a Council meeting. She had also forwarded to Council a tube of fluoride toothpaste bought from an Albury chemist's shop and six copies of a pamphlet called *Why Poison Your Water Supply?* issued by a Sydney vitamin supply firm. Mayor Bunton placed the toothpaste in pride of place on his mayoral rostrum for the whole meeting.

Aunt Faith said you could cut the air in North Albury with a knife. It wasn't every week there was a referendum, and the real people were ready to have their say. Things will change around here now, she said, they are not experimenting on my family. I tried to explain that if she voted No then things would stay the same, but she wasn't having any of it. Mark my words, fluoride will be the beginning of the end. I was staying overnight at her place, although it was mid-week, because Mum was getting worse. We were run off our legs going to Florence's Chemist for Veganin and Relax-a-Tabs. There was no Chateau Tanunda left in the storeroom or under the sink. Mind you, no one said anything, but it was off to Aunt Faith's for the night.

Aunt Faith made Mrs Westie's cooking look plain. The only downside was that Aunt Faith's kids and I had to wash up the plates after dinner with green pine-scented detergent and bright pink rubber gloves. It wasn't too bad if Tom washed and I wiped. Faith spoilt me rotten with her sweets. I even liked her vegetables. She said, what you eat today walks and talks tomorrow. I thought of Mrs Westie and resolved to eat out more. Faith was Mum's sister, and when Mum was a little down she mothered me. The Faiths were big on grace before and after meals, but it was a small price to pay for double helpings of Pavlova and ice cream. I even had a cup of tea after dinner. Boy, I was growing up too fast for my own good.

Aunt Faith was a bit of a Nazi before bed, insisting on brushing my teeth. Tom's were writing pad white. Mine looked like the arse end of matchsticks. When God made teeth he hadn't factored in

Choo-Choo bars, Pavlova and the sucking of sher-
bets. He only allowed for two sets of teeth. A third
set would put Jack Davies out of work, and Uncle
too. Sometimes at Faith's I just ran the tap in the
bathroom so it sounded like I was brushing, and
wet the end of my toothbrush.

Tom's bedroom had two single beds with their
own bedside lamps. It was so much better than the
flashlight I used at home to read by in bed, in the
dark. Uncle Faith didn't have Batman and Phantom
comics like Dad did but some parts of his *Reader's
Digest* were interesting. *Laughter in Uniform* was a
giggle. There was always a volume of *Encyclopedia
Britannica* but I was not strong enough to lift it over
my head and after a while my hand would go to
sleep against my face as I leant on it over the book
lying flat near the pillow. After lights out and some
mumbled prayers led by Aunt Faith, Tom and I
talked about things a bit. I didn't go on in my usual
way because I was really scared shitless that I might
wet the bed. The horror of it all kept me up most of
the night and I woke exhausted but dry in the
morning. With Tom sleeping a few feet away, I had
to be like a thief in the night. I pushed the pillow
down and under me. I humped it with one eye open
and on Tom's silhouette for any movement and the
other closed and thinking of the tartan cushion. It
was too frightening to contemplate boarding school,
where there would be forty boys in one dormitory

with forty pillows and eighty eyes. I'd have to use up my quota of the rubbing before going to Sydney. Is there a set limit to the rubbing? If you stop rubbing for days or weeks or months, does it back up in your willie like the water at the Weir Wall and work its toxic way up your body poisoning your internal organs until it reaches and fries your brain? I'd be safe in Albury from sperm poisoning, but Sydney's a different story.

In the morning Faith said I looked like I was coming down with something. I said I was a bit drained. It was a relief to talk and stop thinking to myself. There really is a God. Aunt Faith's pancakes for breakfast were worth all the prayers and wiping up in the world.

You could walk to school from Tom's, past the wheat silos where after school sometimes we walked through the collected wheat up to our crutches and let it rain down on us from a steel chute, past the empty Showground where thousands had trod days before, past the timberyard of endless buzzing, where sawdust made me sneeze and think of home and the front bar, where Big Jeff Eames spread it on the floor after a bad night. Brother Farrell didn't smile much when I cracked everybody else up by telling him I was handing in my hotelwork. It wasn't technically true since I'd done it at Aunt Faith's but it wasn't time to split hairs. Never let the truth stand between you and a good joke.

Five subjects a day meant five assignments. The Unchristian Brothers must think there's forty hours in a day. It was more than a boy could bear. Brother Farrell said my work was getting better and in fact in the last exams I was fifth in the class. He couldn't believe it. Frankly, neither could I or anyone else. Beginner's luck. A sort of clerical error. But Brother Farrell's face was even more pained than usual, the worry lines that ran across his forehead like a corrugated iron sheet meant something out of the ordinary had happened. He told us that Dag Hammerskjold, the Secretary General of the United Nations, had been killed in a plane crash. I looked at Tom and mouthed Dag. What sort of name was Dag? It turned out he singlehandedly had his finger in the dyke keeping Red Communism in its place and it wouldn't be a surprise to Brother Farrell if they had somehow caused the plane to crash. We said a prayer for his soul, although he was a non-Catholic and now lingering in limbo forever. He'd keep the Communists in their place there.

Brother Farrell said the world was again on the brink. Jesus H. Christ, it was on the brink last week with the disarmament talks breaking down and the Soviets letting off atom bombs in the atmosphere. The Russians were well ahead of the Americans on all fronts and the Yanks' last monkey in space died and was left up there forever circling the Earth. It was more than a boy could understand. At least we had the beer cellar at Waterstreets which we could use if the big ones went off. If there was a warning. Without Dag at the helm the Soviets might just chance it. Any tick of the clock. Only President Kennedy and Mayor Bunton stood in the way. We all quietly prayed for Khrushchev's early death. He didn't look healthy and all that shoe-banging wouldn't do his blood pressure any good. His sudden death wouldn't look suspicious at all.

There wouldn't be room in the cellar for everyone. The newer boarders could look after themselves. Taillight and his family were okay but Mr Stephens would have to empty his pipe. Everyone in the class would have to be extra nice if they wanted shelter. There was no way Tibor Toth could fit in. Hayden Sir Sir Livermore would luck his way in. Mrs Westie would have to cook from cans, which might be better, considering. Mr Stephens would bring all his guns in case of invasion. Oh Jesus Mary and Joseph, keep the Communists out of Albury and I'll never do the rubbing again.

The panic evaporated as quickly as it had set in. By lunchtime life resumed at Aquinas as if Dag was still with us, but every now and again his name would cross my mind and I'd shudder. The world was changing, and so was I. The big question was, was it for the better or the worse. We'd soon find out, perhaps in a big white flash like Nagasaki, and all that would be standing would be the Civic Theatre and the Albury Railway Station. And the balcony at Waterstreets. You grew up quicker under the threats of the Red Peril and the Yellow Plague. If there was one thing worse than a Communist it must be a Chinese Communist. They wanted us badly. If you looked at a map, just gravity would carry them down to Australia, then to Albury. Would I denounce God under bayonet point? Probably, but I'd cross my fingers or my eyes or legs. Oh, the pressure. The pressure.

Mum wasn't going to make the Albury Public School Hall to vote. She was still under room arrest upstairs. She'd have to vote absentee. Maybe she could vote twice. The Spring Show had about done her in. Aunt Faith says Mum thinks too much. She also tells me that the world doesn't owe me a living. Sure thing. Who asked anyway.

You couldn't tell it was referendum day by looking out the bedroom window of room 17. It looked like every other day when it was sunny and clear, magpies calling each other names from leafy plane trees in Smollett Street. Jimmy B had picked up the *Border* and was giving it the once-over before sending it up to Dad. No one can tell if someone else has read your newspaper before you, if you're real careful. I wish I could vote, Jimmy. Oh, yes, and which way would you go then? I don't know, but I still wish I could vote.

Jimmy B had no kids and regarded voting or too much thinking as an unwarranted interference with his Saturday. However, he had real strong views on the Council seat by-election that was taking place at the same time. He fancied Max Luff who worked next door at Albury Border Transport. He was standing on a platform comprising anti-fluoridation, support for the building of North Albury baths, beautification of the cemetery but against the removal of headstones from graves, and for extension of sewerage services to South and West Albury. It was a pretty unbeatable combina-tion of issues, I thought. He sometimes popped into the back bar after work, making him Waterstreets' first City Council candidate customer.

Jimmy B cackled out loud and plonked his off-white enamel mug hard on the marble top of Mrs Westie's kitchen table, sprinkling hot tea over both of us. Sorry Charlie but this really breaks me up, he said, pointing to an inside page of the *Border*. The bloody Council has finally been flushed out, he cried as we brushed each other down with tea towels. Five aldermen had declared their sacred and secret votes on fluoridation. It was five against and two for. In fact, two had flip-flopped from their earlier statements. Alderman Garland had broken the ice and said he wouldn't be told what to eat and drink. Ald Batrouney said he read everything and couldn't make up his mind, so he was voting No. The young Ald Garland Jr said all the information was a series of opposites and followed his father. Mayor Bunton finally declared he was always against it. He couldn't say it didn't prevent decay, but worried about other abnormalities. They all decried the recent radio debate as regrettable because of personal attacks by certain unnamed persons.

Jimmy B smoothed the paper out with his hands and gave it the once over with the bottom of the kettle off the stove to iron out suspicious creases. Mrs Westie was making up a breakfast tray for Mum and Dad. Mum's would come back untouched except for the bacon rashers Dad pinched. Breakfast can be too confronting for someone in Mum's condition. Dad tended to lie in a bit on weekends because of the late nights. Every day was a weekend for Mum lately.

Big Jeff had opened the bar early for the first brigade of nervous voters. They really were Albury's movers and shakers. There wasn't much going on there, so I checked upstairs. Dad was eating from his tray in the lounge room and the bedroom door was locked. I stepped over the Hood in the hallway and went out on to the front verandah. You could see the entire length of Smollett Street down to the pool and up to the station on a day like this.

I stuck my head around the side and looked to the roof at the red and green neon sign that winked Waterstreets Hotel day and night in running writing. It made me feel ten feet tall to see the family name in neon. I loved to glance at it. It's very reassuring, and lets you know who you are and where you're from, except when some of the letters went on the blink. On the corner opposite Taillight's, behind windows covered by rainbow-striped canvas blinds, lived the Duckworths. If you'd looked up from the footpath you would have seen me with Dad's big racing binoculars trained for any movement in or out of the house by fourteen-year-old blonde-haired brown-eyed luscious Diana Duckworth. The magic of magnification was as close as I got, but I knew every blackhead and pimple on her fabulous face. I once took a pile of comics to her place to swap, but she wasn't home. Thank Christ. On the balcony with field glasses was as close as I really wanted to come. She'd ride her bike, lifting her blue high school tunic up her fuzzy downy thighs with each push up and down on the foot pedals. Every now and again I'd look up Duckworth in the Albury and District phone book and just thrill to the name. I'd ring and hang up. Heaven knows what I'd say. Nothing. There wasn't anything to say. She was more your visual experience. She was a walking and talking wet dream.

Mum called out a croaky Charles for me so I

snuck back into the lounge with Dad for protection from any mission or message to the pharmacy or downstairs. He was listening to Punters Racing Roundup on the radio, marking the tips 1, 2, 3 in order, and writing in late jockey changes and weights and ruling out scratchings. The punting was not a game of luck but of infinite possibilities for the well-informed. Dad was tapped into information from everywhere except the horse itself. The phone rang off the hook on Saturday mornings with the late oil from boozy jockeys and Dad's top secret contacts in all the major capital cities. They'd say It's me when I picked up the phone. They gave no names, for fear of the eavesdropper. By the time Dad went downstairs the paper had more handwriting on it than printing. He rolled the Melbourne papers, the *Saturday Sporting Globe* and the *Border* into a giant round bundle and put it as deep as he could into a side pocket of his trousers. He spent the afternoon unholstering them many times over. A punter's work is never done until the last race from Adelaide, which was half an hour behind East Coast/Albury time. Mr Stephens had an aerial wrapped around his home to pick up the interstate races. Some bastards conned him by splicing a tape recorder into his electricity and betting on winners they heard earlier, before his time-delayed broadcast. You couldn't trust anyone these days.

Katherine Ann was born for the stage. She was born on the day Wodalla won the Melbourne Cup and Dad had to wait for the last race to jump on the *Spirit of Progress* to get back to Albury. Already at seven she'd won Chickabidees, Holdenson and Neilson's Singing Competition on 2AY and the Albury Eisteddfod. I was angling to manage her next year with ten per cent of the take. There was nothing she couldn't do – singing, dancing, tap, mime, the lot. The shelf above the fireplace and under the Green Indonesian Woman had so many of Katherine Ann's trophies it looked like the front window of the Swift Sheet Pawn Shop. When she wasn't at school she was in constant audition. Her whole life was a rehearsal for something. Downstairs the Ladies Lounge was empty but ready for the big day ahead. Katherine Ann was playing the upright butt-burnt piano and giving *Silent Night* the jazzy touch.

Musical ability was like a magic trick to me. I wasn't tone deaf because I loved listening but more tone dumb. Brother Farrell had twisted my ear at choir practice when he inspected row after row of hymn-singing boys by running his turned head along us like a xylophone. Words and music just came out of my mouth like the sound of a go-kart. All would be well I hoped when my voice broke.

Piano playing was a small miracle. In Katherine Ann's hands it was a wand. In mine a stick. Even drunks on their last legs late in the night could stagger into the Ladies Lounge, plonk down on the stool and play some classical music, music without words, Dad called it, that you only ever heard on 2CO the local ABC radio station. The piano was all Greek to me. Watching Katherine Ann all I could see was black, black, white, black, white, white, black, black, black, white, black, black. How anyone did it only Heaven knows.

A couple of the womenfolk had entered with full mid-morning sherries on a silver tray and taken up positions in the front stalls. I left them looking at each other, isn't she wonderful, beautiful dress, what a talent, all that stuff. Maybe God only gives you one talent. Katherine Ann couldn't shoot a slug gun straight if her life depended on it.

Every door of the Public and Saloon Bars was open, letting sunlight tinge the cigarette smoke like thunderclouds after rain. A rainbow almost arched through the bars. The atmosphere was hydroelectric. Dad was organising the Punters' Club selections for the day. Unfortunately for the club it was Uncle's turn to pick the racecard. Jack Davies tried to translate Uncle's picks. Uncle loved rank outsiders. Jack's entreaties for at least some favourites fell on deaf ears. Dad wrote Uncle's choices on the Carlton and United Melbourne Bitter blackboard to the groans of club members. Imagine if one wins, cheered Dad. We could buy the pub, said Jack

Davies. Uncle laughed. It was early in the day.

Mr and Mrs McEvoy had already voted on their way to Waterstreets. They were regulars on Saturday mornings. She sat on her own in the Ladies Lounge, listening to something she thought sounded like *Silent Night* but was too fast, wasn't it, and sipped brandy lime and soda with a touch of bitters. Mr McEvoy rested his wide frame over a totally inadequate stool in the Public Bar. They liked to get the morning's shopping, toiletries and compulsory voting out of the way before they settled into the serious business at hand at Waterstreets. Most of the other regulars did not have voting high on their minds. They could pop down to the public school on one of the trips to Mr Stephens' during the afternoon. Many would vote informal or not at all. It was a waste when you considered the number of Anzac Day marches I raced up the side lane to attend to ensure the right to vote.

Dad asked me to help behind the bar. Big Jeff was run off his elephant legs. I wrapped a Waterstreets Hotel tea towel around my waist and picked up seven-ounce glasses two at a time to fill. Looks like a dress, said Captain Jack Saunders (retired). My shiny white legs were held in place by mismatched socks in plastic sandals. Get out of it, I replied quick as a flash.

When people bought a bottle of beer or plonk to

take away Dad insisted that they were properly wrapped in old newspaper tucked in with hospital corners so that other people in the street wouldn't take offence at someone holding alcohol. It also protected the contents a little if as often happened you dropped them. The footpath down Smollett Street was potted late on Saturday nights with wet newspaper, broken glass and teardrops.

Saturday mornings were always fresh and busy. Everyone was determined to enjoy their day off. Even the unemployed. Saturdays held unlimited potential. It was a poor fool's paradise. Sunday morning waited unseen around the kerb with its big stick. After an hour I was getting antsy and Dad let me out through the hinged counter of the bar at the end. I burst out the front door gasping for breath. With all the smoke I'd be lucky to grow another inch.

The morning was almost over and I hadn't done a worthwhile thing so I skipped to Taillight's quickly, not to waste any more time. Taillight had his head in the engine of the Super Snipe. The car bonnet was held up with a long thin green piece of metal and parts of what I took to be the engine were scattered across the yard. Taillight looked like one of the Negro Minstrels that had recently played the Civic Theatre. He wore a white T-shirt with the sleeves rolled up right to his shoulders. He had a packet of cigarettes twisted into each sleeve. It gave the appearance of big shoulders. His cigarette habit was getting out of hand. His T-shirt looked like a police fingerprint form.

There was nothing wrong with the car. Taillight just liked taking it apart and putting it back together. He sometimes got it right but the mechanic from Albury Border Transport was only a holler away. This was not my idea of thrilling, but exciting company and things to do were thin on the ground on weekends in Smollett Street. There was always a chance Diana Duckworth would saunter by and see me fixing up a car. Taillight pointed out the parts of the Super Snipe engine by name. They just didn't stick. I knew the capital of every country, the rainfall of every major city in the State and all the Melbourne Cup winners by heart, but the word carburettor went in one ear and out the other. It was like making mental notes with nothing to write on. The car and its components were way outside my vocabulary. I accepted this as Uncle did his deafness and admired Taillight the more.

After a time I suggested in turn fishing, swimming, dropping pebbles off the railway bridge, making gunpowder, doing a Deanie. All were met with a lazy Maybe later, maybe later. There was no doubt about it. Taillight was a different boy. I couldn't work out what had got into him. Maybe it was a passing virus which he'd soon shrug off and we'd be up the old Union Bridge jumping, him headfirst me feetfirst, into the Mighty Murray, suddenly remembering how frigging freezing it was, and being swept into Norieul Park. I hoped he'd get over it in time.

Taillight had his stereophonic hi-fi plugged into a series of long electric extension cords through the front window and playing an LP of Elvis Presley at full blast. He knew every word, every move, every lip curl. As soon as it stopped he'd rush over and lift the diamond-studded stereo arm back across the record with a loud scratching sound and play it all over again. He was dancing to the beat of a different drummer. I wasn't playing with him of late. I was watching him play by himself. He was leaving me behind in his wake. The evidence lay in the buffalo grass all around his yard. All the unpronounceable parts of his father's car. There was no use trying to feign interest. Taillight had a trained bullshit detector. He had slipped out of the ginger beer generation and into the brown beer generation when I wasn't looking. Jesus H. Christ. He would be voting himself soon.

He promised to go to the Dairy Queen with me after lunch to play pinball. He believed they made Dairy Queen ice cream with paint thinner. I said ta ta and drifted back home in search of the pick of Mrs Westie's counter lunches.

The front bar was bursting on to the street with boozers. People seemed more pissed than usual for Saturday lunchtime. It was the tension and excitement of the referendum. The future of my teeth was in their hands. When things got tough people needed to put their worries behind them. That's why Menzies Bloody Credit Squeeze was not an entirely terrible thing for the pub business. There was always some money for the drink, even when there was no money for jam.

Although counter lunch was part of the week's paid accommodation, most of the permanent boarders did not avail themselves of it on Saturdays. If they thought of it, it was after 2.30 in the afternoon and Mrs Westie would slam the wire screen kitchen door in their faces and cry it was too late and she'd put it all back in the fridge. They stumbled back to the bar humbled and hungry, ordering potato chips and peanuts.

We all ate sausages in onion sauce with mashed potatoes one veg in the kitchen. John, Peter and the Hood threw food at each other. Katherine Ann hummed. I read Mrs Westie's *Women's Weekly* from top to tail, resting it on the salt and pepper shakers. The waitress Florence carried trays of steaming plates back and forth to the front of the hotel. Dad's clear instruction to Mrs Westie was to put plenty of salt in all the dishes. Wink wink. Unlike Uncle she didn't need to be told things twice. We sold plenty of beers in the afternoons after counter lunch.

The *Women's Weekly* covered affairs of state outside Albury. In fact Albury was hardly ever mentioned, and when it was Aunt Faith was on the phone to Mum with the page reference. There were pages of the latest fashions in frocks, coloured pictures of parties in progress with people holding cocktails high, Mandrake the Magician, and the latest story of Princess Margaret, who I didn't care all that much for. In fact I booed when she came on to the screen with the Queen in the film clip at the end of pictures at the Regent. My favourite was the Princess Alexandra who smiled at me from the back of a Jeep at the Jubilee in the Sports Ground when visiting Albury. She'd married Lord Ogilvie, lucky bugger. I was sure she'd remember me. They dined on galah soup the night they stayed in Albury. Mrs Carnegie said it took 24 galahs to make the soup.

While we ate Jimmy B put up a dozen streamers of fly paper which he gently tacked into the ceiling with the bottom of his shoes. Spring was upon us and so came the blowies. Before long specks appeared on the fly paper and by Christmas Day they would be black, thick with dead flies, like black streamers hanging over the dining tables. Mrs Westie carried a plastic fly swat in one hand all winter and summer. Just for the practice in the off-season.

★ ★ ★

The afternoon stretched out endlessly before me. There's nothing to do, I complained to Dad. Hmmm. There's never anything to do. Hmmm. Can't I go to the pictures? Mum said I could. Instantly I knew I had taken one step too far. Dad asked when did she say that. Couple of days ago. Hmmm. He pulled all his chins into his neck and inclined his forehead towards me and peered through his eyebrows. Hmmmm. He took a couple of shillings out of his pocket and flicked them in the air as if playing two-up. Dad is a god. I trousered them immediately and made my way to Taillight's.

I practically had to drag him to the Dairy Queen. There was no use revealing to him the full extent of my recent wealth because he'd only put the lot through the pinball machine. I secretly kept enough for the Regent and a Jersey toffee bar. Mind you, if pinballs paid like pokies Taillight would have been a rich man. But pinballs were one way traffic coinwise. Taillight had the knack of bumping the machine without registering tilt – an art form missing in lesser mortals. Once, at the Boomerang Café, the machine ran out of numbers and it had to start adding up all over again. He was only on his second ball. He was jumping and bumping the Indy 500 machine until I was red in the face with exhaustion. When it was my turn the balls just seemed destined to go straight down the middle, out of arm's way.

Some girl called Monica came over and talked to us, or more particularly to Taillight. I knew when I wasn't wanted and said ta ta and went over the road to the Regent. It was another Jungle Jim double feature. Halfway through the first feature I still couldn't tell if I'd seen it before. I wrapped half the toffee bar in paper for the second feature. Some aspects of the theatre business were beyond me. Front stalls, for example, were half the cost of back stalls. Why? They were easily the best seats in the house, way up close to the screen. You'd think they would be more expensive. And another thing. They paid good money to ushers to work, when there'd be hundreds of kids willing to pay for that job. Taillight had once made a fortune selling pass-outs, until they started switching colours to stamp it out.

Jungle Jim Part II could have been the same picture as before Intermission. The cheeky bloody monkey got right up my nose and I bit down on a piece of silver paper with a filling and got a shock that nearly sent me through the skygarden and waterfall roof.

The whole business put me in a deep hole and I left the premises before The End came on to the screen for the first time in my life. Maybe the shock reminded me of Mum's troubles and treatment. Normally I watched the Queen's clip to the last frame, but there was a restless anxiety around the town itself which must have got into the Regent's air-conditioning.

Monica was sitting in the front seat of the Humber with Taillight when I got home. He was driving her round and round the block. The mechanic must have helped get the car started. They waved as they drove up Smollett Street at 20 mph. He didn't ask me to join them. Who'd want to anyway. Taillight understood the ways of girls the way I knew the back of my own hand. He told me that his working motto with them was old enough to smoke, old enough to poke.

The railway workers were well into their shift, two or three sheets to the wind. I didn't mind going up to the station to bundy them off work, but when they asked if I'd run up to the public school hall and vote for them I knew for sure they were having a lend of me. The shunters were great leg pullers from way back. They sent telegrams to people all over Albury congratulating them on winning the Opera House lottery. It was okay because the people they sent them to deserved it. That is, they didn't deserve to win the lottery.

After the last race there was only ten minutes until voting closed and Dad asked if I wanted to go with him. It was only two blocks but Dad never walked anywhere. Jack Davies and Uncle looked at him then at each other, got off their stools and motioned to go with us. Ernie Carpenter put a hook up to come. Captain Jack Saunders (retired) saluted as we passed him and fell in behind. Dad pulled J-J-Jack S-S-Shiebs off the back stairs where he was having a little shut-eye and we all scrambled into the Holden in the back yard. We bowled down the lane in a cloud of dust and smoke. The closest parking spot we could get after circling all over was in front of our own pub, so we all ended up walking anyway. The Waterstreets were renowned latecomers, whether it was church, the railway, visiting relatives, our own funerals or whatever.

Dad rushed in exactly at closing time and gave his name, breathless, to a man sitting at a school desk with a long list of printed names in a file in front of him, holding a ruler. One by one, he ruled out the names. Mrs Kathleen Waterstreet won't be able to vote today. She's sick. You'll need to send a medical certificate, with the condition and date of illness, to the Town Clerk first thing on Monday or there will be a fine. Dad nodded and got two bits of paper and a two-inch-long shaved pencil. It was so small it kept falling out of his hand when he made his mark. When I tried to look under his shoulder he used his bum to gently nudge me out of the way. It's a secret ballot, he smiled. I knew anyway. Dad was loyal to his customers and would never vote against the mayor's wishes. Mayor Bunton stood like a colossus across the Mighty Murray River, with one foot on Monument Hill in Albury and the other in the hollow that is Wodonga. The cold waters of the Weir ran between his legs.

Ernie Carpenter had trouble not only with the pencil but staying on his feet. The man with the ruler said that all the Jacks and Uncle were too drunk to vote. Jack Davies leaned over the table and demanded to know where the by-law was that said there was a limit to the amount of alcohol that a voter could consume. To the man with the ruler all the Jacks looked like beanstalk giants. Voices were raised, names were taken, but eventually little pencils were handed out, with two slips each. Everyone staggered about, looking for the box to sit on. Jack Shiebs was startled to find himself in a school hall and not asleep on the back stairs, where he distinctly recalled having a little rest. When he thought to himself he didn't stutter. He would do a lot more of the thinking in the future, he resolved. A lifetime on the edge had taught him there were no surprises left. The Captain wept when he realised the enormous responsibility that was cast upon him. Dad helped him through. I helped Ernie fill in his ballot by gently guiding his hook and pencil. But the bugger wanted to vote against Max Luff and for Clive Westhorp. It was a tug of war. The pencil made big streaks along the form. We had to get another. Again I fought with him on fluoridation.

His hook kept wanting to mark No and I Yes. Eventually I let him have it his way. It was his vote. It was just my teeth.

The voting had worked up a great thirst, and Jack Davies shouted the whole bar when, triumphantly, we returned.

Fifteen potato

The *Border Morning Mail* reported in bold and big headlines that NO FLUORIDE IS VOICE OF PUBLIC in equal billing with a photo of a mounted soldier and his horse on one side of the page and CLIFF FALL FATAL on the other. The No vote won in a clear waterslide. By Monday's counting, 6902 had voted against fluoridation and a mere 1771 for. The whole Anti-Fluoridation Committee saw Mr J.E. Harding off at Albury Railway Station where he began the return journey to Rockhampton. Dr Hogan, on behalf of the Fluoridation Committee, said the campaign had been an interesting one and in general fair. Of the 2975 No votes cast at the Public School, Dad's had been one. He had finally backed a winner. Or so it seemed.

Life briefly returned to abnormal. All the Jacks,

Uncles and Ernie Carpenters of Albury had spoken.

The shit hit the fan on Wednesday, 27 September 1961. The *Sydney Morning Herald*, the most important organ in Australia, published an editorial on the previous Saturday's referendum:

> By referendum, the people of Albury have voted decisively against fluoridation of their water supply. That, of course, is their right in a democratic community, if given the chance. The Albury City Council, for understandable reasons, felt impelled to give them that chance. In a relatively small community, stirred up by propagandists from other parts of Australia, perhaps no other decision could have been expected, and it is futile for the Health Department to express disapproval of such referenda no matter how deplorable the results may be – as they certainly are in this case.
>
> The people of Albury have gone on record as insisting on the sacred right to let their own teeth – and, more importantly, those of their children – rot. Very well, then: let them take the consequences. They must pay for this 'freedom'. If there is any sign of support in Albury for a Government-sponsored dental benefits scheme, nobody will pay any attention. Indeed, if a dental

benefits scheme ever becomes a practical proposition, communities which reject fluoridation of their water supplies should be specifically excluded from it. Then there might be an agonising reappraisal of anti-fluoridation arguments.

The case for fluoridation of community water supplies is overwhelming, and it is depressing that there should be so many cranks who oppose it with such passionate intensity. Reason seems to fly out of the window in any public discussion of the issue – and not just in Australia. But the lesson of Albury is surely this: that Health Departments, medical and dental authorities cannot expect their strong pro-fluroidation arguments to win by default, for the forces of unreason are alarmingly strong. Whenever the issue arises, the experts must get out and fight from the beginning. Great is truth, and it shall prevail. Perhaps! But only if it is given the chance.

The town was in what Aunt Faith described as high dudgeon for most of October. If anything, the attacks from the capital cities and their lackies bonded the town together more than fluoride ever could. There was a general air of up yours.

As everyone knows, the 23rd of October is the anniversary of the landing of the Dutch plane *Univer* at Albury Racecourse. In the 1934 London to Melbourne Centenary Air Race, the Dutch plane got hopelessly lost in terrible weather between Charleville (no relation) and Melbourne. In the middle of the night Captain Parmentier and his trusty navigator Moll saw the glittering lights of Albury and circled the town in constant contact with Radio Station 2CO at nearby Corowa. But there was a problem. Despite the very long train platform, Albury town planners hadn't gotten around to building an aerodrome. So the call went out over 2CO at midnight for anybody with a vehicle to drive to Albury Racecourse. It was a lucky thing that anyone was awake at that hour. Albury's emergency services were very worried about the safety of the Monument Hill because the Dutch aren't used to mountains. Holland is as flat as a tack. When Grandpa Waterstreet got there in his Model-T Ford he was ushered by the race stewards into a huge line of other cars with their headlights shining on to the straight. Captain Parmentier and Moll dropped brilliant parachute flares, so illuminating the racecourse that Dad said they could have run the Sodens Hotel Albury Cup then and there. The *Univer* made a perfect landing on the straight to greet the judges just past the finishing post.

The next day Grandpa helped unload the plane

of all its mail and pulled it out of the bog, leaving the Albury Racecourse with one of the most treacherous straights in the State. None of the passengers or mail was allowed back on and the *Univer* took off into the wind at a hundred miles per hour and came second in the Air Race.

The Dutch people were over the moon with Albury and the then mayor was appointed to the Order of Orange-Nassau by Queen Wilhelmina herself. In the Town Council chamber sits a plaque to this very day, in words and pictures, commemorating Grandpa and the others' epic feat of 23 October 1934. Unfortunately, the *Univer* crashed into a little mountain which they didn't see coming the next year and the people of Albury reciprocated by donating a memorial in Holland to those lost. It was tit for tat.

But the whole kerfuffle led to people thinking that the place needed its very own aerodrome. If you wanted to fly you had to drive to Corowa. So before you knew it, in just thirty years plus of planning, work had commenced in early 1961 on the Albury Aerodrome. The ever-grateful Dutch people donated a disused KLM Douglas aeroplane which was the spitting image of the one that landed on the racecourse and later crashed. Mayor Bunton and the aldermen had it mounted on a big steel pipe at a slight angle to the ground near the entrance of the soon to be commenced public carpark at the

Albury Aerodrome. It sits there, frozen in time, as a tribute to the town before it joined the space race. I think my cousin Tom might have had a hand in sticking it in place.

So Dad's dad was a bit of a hero for a while, but he died suddenly when Dad was exactly my age, eleven. Since I've turned eleven I keep a hawk's eye on Dad to make sure he's okay. History has a funny way of repeating itself. You can't have two sick parents or we'll all be lining up at St John's Orphanage under the lash of Uncle Bob's leather straps wielded by the Sisters Without Mercy.

I know a bit of the hero rubbed off on Dad and I hope there's enough to rub off on me. When Dad's dad died the sportswriter at the *Border* wrote a personal obituary describing Mr Waterstreet as the whitest man I knew. That's the sort of stuff that gushes in my veins. The *Border* said he was one of Albury's great sportsmen, owning a string of greyhounds including the unofficial world record holder over hurdles for 400 yards. A photo of Royal Buzz's unclocked win in that race holds pride of place over the pool table in the Saloon Bar. In those days you only had to own dogs or racehorses to be a sportsman. It's much tougher nowadays.

By early November much of the steam had gone out of the referendum furore and Albury's attention spanned to the big one, the Melbourne Cup. The first Tuesday of every November for 101 years, the traffic stopped to a standstill on Dean Street, shoppers stopped shopping, workers stopped working, public servants stopped whatever they were doing, and even schoolboys stopped daydreaming at 3 p.m. Heaven knows what they did before radio. The Aborigines must have used smoke signals between Melbourne and Albury over the Dandenongs to call the race. In this year of Our Lord the race would be broadcast live on television in Mates's window in perfect black and white.

The placing of bets on racehorses was illegal outside the racecourse, excepting on Melbourne Cup Day when there was a temporary ceasefire between the punter and the police. Captain Jack Saunders (retired) said of his first campaign in Gallipoli that the Anzacs and the Turks would stop shooting at each other by agreement for two hours each day so they could remove the dead from the field and then start all over again. The bodies must have got in the way of a good shot. Well, the police wanted to place a bet on Cup Day.

Every business worth its name in Albury had a Melbourne Cup sweep, but there was no sweep bigger than Streets Annual Orphanage Appeal Sweep. Technically, it was not legal. Even the learned Harry Flood couldn't find a loophole with either of his eagle eyes. But the Chief Secretary in Sydney in charge of the punting, vice and drugs in the State turned a blind eye himself to the sweeps on Melbourne Cup Day, without even getting a half-dozen bottles in the boot of his car. The orphanage in question was St John's Orphanage in Thurgoona, another satellite town of Albury about two miles from the GPO. The Sisters Without Mercy had run it since Kingdom Come for kids without parents or parents affected by the booze and stuff. Albury parents always threatened Albury kids with the orphanage. But that was a bit like Brer Rabbit, the Fox and the Briar Patch.

Dad's dad, Charles Christian Waterstreet the First, had started the Orphanage Appeal Sweep in the 1920s and it had become an institution by the time Dad took it over. Streets sweep is a unique form of the punting. You buy a ticket – there's thousands sold – and 24 lucky people's names are picked out of a barrel and matched to the 24 horses set to race in the Melbourne Cup. It includes reserves so you might get a horse but unless there's a scratching you mightn't get a start. More than two-thirds of the money collected goes to the orphanage, and the rest, less than a third by my new slide rule, is divided up between 1st, 2nd, 3rd and last placegetters. Like a referendum, it is democracy in action. Even the losers win.

My Grandpa Waterstreet died years before I was born and was buried in the Catholic portion of Albury Cemetery with a big headstone. Taillight and I loved going there. I would lie on the marble slab with the headstone over me with the same name as mine, radiating out like Our Lady's halo. Taillight would pretend he was Henry Arthur Collins, died 1892, In Loving Memory by his wife Violet Louise Collins neé Fretwell. We'd walk around the cemetery with our arms extended, eyes half closed, moaning, running into trees and each other, scaring the life out of the barely living tending the flower pots on the plots of their dearly beloved. We hadn't done that for a while.

Anyway, Grandpa Waterstreet started this tradition and it raised thousands of pounds for the kids every year. It got bigger and bigger. Dad would have Albury Printing Press make thousands of sweep tickets in grey books of ten, which would be on prominent display and sale in all Albury's businesses, big and small. It was Streets because Waterstreets was too long to print on the stub. It may have been to put the Chief Secretary off the scent if he changed his tack. I walked sky high in my sandals at the Dairy Queen, Hume Weir Café, even Mates, wherever I spied the grey ticket books of Streets Orphanage Appeal Sweep held by a piece of string to the shop counters. Even Aunt Faith, who knew nothing about horse racing and thought jockeys had no sense of colour, would join in, buying tickets and even, God forbid, placing a bet, which I'm sure she'd confess immediately by telephone to

Father Bongiorno before the race.

In the weeks before the Cup, Dad would load the Holden with a big box of ticket books and take them from shop to shop. Some of your up-market ladies fashion shops shook their heads at such goings on and refused to let Dad leave a book or two. I thought they'd rot in hell. Dad just said it was horses for courses and let it be.

At the same time, 2AY had a country and western singing competition for locals who fancied themselves. Every morning the station would play a couple of tape recordings, usually made in the bathroom, of potential stars and voters would write in with their favourite. The winner got a recording contract and a return train trip to Sydney. It was a musical example of democracy in action. Tommy Meehan who played in Waterstreets was my favourite. They all sang their own songs that they themselves had written. It was very hard to tell the difference between them. There is no good news in country and western songs. Overnight and in the morning people became stars. Les Kerangan whose closest brush with fame was to have his name in running writing on the driver's side door of his truck with its loaded and unloaded weight suddenly became a household name from Jindera to Yackandandah. Albury was abuzz with the country and western

music and the Melbourne Cup. I voted for Tommy
many times in entirely different handwriting.

One of the things I love best is thinking about
stuff I did as a kid. I really look forward to looking
back. So when I was driving around with Dad,
dropping off sweep tickets, sticking up posters, it
got me to thinking about when we had the grocery
shop for a couple of years, before Dad got the pub
under Grandpa's will and Nana bought her own
pub down the other end of Smollett Street. At the
shop, Dad would deliver newspapers from his Austin A40. Very early in the morning, the *Border
Morning Mail* truck dropped a bundle of *Borders* off
with a thump in front of the shop, smelling of warm
wood. Dad would cut the wire and roll each *Border*
like a giant roll-your-own cigarette. Mum was in
great fettle then. She would cut up bike tyre tubes
into black rubber bands and slip them over the
paper baton Dad had made. Then we'd all grab an
armful of papers like kindling and drop them into
the front passenger seat of the Austin. Dad would
drive slowly down David Street, Townsend Street,
Macauley Street, wherever he had the run, and
throw a stick of newspaper like a straight boomerang into the front yards of customers. If he missed
the porch, I'd scamper out the back seat and open
the gate and put it safely near the front door away
from the irritating frost or stray dog. Sometimes I
jogged next to the Austin like an athlete. They were

the days, I thought. Things change. Stuff seemed simpler then.

Mum was out for the count at this time. Before she took to the bed, we'd gone to the Boys Department at Mates and Mr Chamberlain measured me for a new school uniform for Waverley College next year. He sent the measurements to David Jones in Sydney, who eventually sent me a blue uniform with gold striping, three blue shirts, two pairs of woollen socks, and about fifty printed name tags to be sewn on to every item of clothing I owned. Otherwise I might end up wearing some creep's underpants at boarding school. Mum wasn't big on sewing so Mrs Westie did it by hand between meals. C.C. Waterstreet in red cotton print. Maybe not in neon lights but I felt a bit like a somebody myself. Everything on me bore my name. I hoped the dye didn't run on the pyjamas if I wet the bed. There were two months to go and the bedwetting still kept me up at night. Dr Mackenzie's Sensor was next to useless and used a fortune in batteries.

People studied the form guide of Cup runners as if it were final exams. Housewives who wouldn't know one end of a horse from another told neighbours that Lennox Walker had predicted rain for the Cup and you've got to watch those New Zealand horses in the mud. It was wetter than Melbourne in New Zealand. They loved the mud over there. Mr Stephens had to get a bunch of new pencils to keep up with the punting. Even the Unchristian Brothers fancied a bet on the Cup. Last year at 3 p.m. Social Studies stopped and the Bakelite was whooped up full volume and everyone in the class cracked rulers on their backsides all the way down the straight. It was the 100th anniversary of the Cup and a bolter at 50 to 1 got up. Everyone was down for a while after that. Hi Jinx was from New Zealand.

Somewhere in Australia Ursula was making a tidy sum from her crystal ball. She'd know the winner for sure. Cup fever gripped Albury like nothing since the referendum. There were more experts than punters. You'd think every one of the horses was going to win if you listened to everyone carefully.

Tempers got a little frayed just before Cup Day. With Mum upstairs, Dad had to do all the counting and ticketing himself. Big Jeff Eames wasn't much help. The small printing was beyond his bottlo glasses. I helped after homework. Aunt Faith came over to lend a hand, and once she lost her temper at the waitress who was miscounting some of the coins delivered in boxes from a shop downtown. We're not running a charity here, she bawled. Well we were, I thought, but it really was hectic and everyone was frantic.

Dad said we weren't allowed to buy tickets for

the sweep ourselves. It would look bad if a Waterstreet won. So I agreed with Taillight and bought a
bundle of tickets in his name but in my handwriting.
We'd go halves if we won. I put his real name down.
Basil Stephens. I'm not completely stupid, whatever
you've heard.

The favourite was Sparkler ridden by Jack
Purtle. That was the horse people wanted to draw.
The next favourite was the Victorian Derby winner,
Dhaulagiri with a silent h. High on everyone's list
were Sky High and Blue Era who had fought out
the New South Wales Derby neck and neck and
one jockey had tried to dislodge the other all the
way down the straight by lifting his leg. He'd
forgotten that film had been introduced about 20
years earlier. Some jockeys don't have it up there
for thinking.

Although Dad really loved the wee people as he
called jockeys and was always sticking up for the
little man, there were some wee people who had let
us down. At one Albury race meeting Vic was
indisposed and Dad engaged another local rider for
the Court. The Court was leading by six lengths as
they turned into the straight but the jockey stood up
in the saddle and put on the brakes and the Court
was beaten again by a nose. Dad had put a fortune
of the takings on the Court and was furious and
rushed into the jockeys' room to punch him out or
at least give him a father of a hiding. The jockey had

already left the racecourse in Dad's silks. He had been bribed by the bookies. A couple of days later we were motoring down Swift Street in the Holden when Dad sighted the jockey. There's Better Brakes he yelled and turned the Holden on to the footpath and chased the jockey all the way down Swift Street to the canal, where he escaped. Mum kept crying out Bill, Bill. The jockey certainly ran faster than the Court did down the straight. The lesson, Dad said, is that some of the wee people haven't got it up there for thinking. If the Court had won I'd have tipped him triple what the bookies paid him.

The draw was in the front bar at about 8 o'clock on Cup Eve. Dad would then rush down to Albury Printing and would quickly get a number of sheets of the lucky holders of horse tickets run off and deliver them to all the shops. The *Border* wouldn't print it for fear of the Chief Secretary. The pub was chokablock. Dad emptied all the tickets into a huge empty oil drum. Mrs McEvoy did the honours and Dad read out each lucky name and matched it with each horse in the race. There were a few false cheers every time a Jack someone won, but none of our Jacks got a horse. Neither did Taillight. You'd think Dad could at least fudge me a horse. It didn't need to be a favourite. What are fathers for?

After all the hoopla, I went upstairs to study the Turf Guide for myself. I'd always fancied outsiders. I guess it was the Irish in me. Rooting for the underhorse. I decided to be scientific about it. Since I was going to Sydney next year, I'd pick a Sydney horse. No one ever expected them to win. the Sydney races ran in the opposite direction to Melbourne races. The almighty government might interfere with the railway gauges but they'd never touch the ponies for fear of upsetting the balance of things and the bookies. I rang Mr Stephens first thing the next day before school and had five bob each way on Lord Fury. At 3.10 p.m. that afternoon my bottom was red raw with ruler marks after Lord Fury led all the way at 20 to 1.

The Court of Petty Sessions luckily sat in the morning when Harry Flood was at his peak, before lunch, and upheld Dad's appeal. Dad kept his licence and Mum wouldn't have to put her name over the front door as licencee. Tommy nearly won the country and western competition.

Things were looking up.

Sixteen potato

The summer flew through Albury as quickly as the Interstate Daylight Express on the new standard gauge. Mum had worn out her welcome at all the Melbourne hospitals and went to Sydney for some nerve treatment. She missed Christmas with us, but most of all she missed Mrs Westie's famous Christmas pudding. The great secret to Mrs Westie's Christmas pud was to give it plenty of time to mature. It was like Barney Gehrig's wine, which needed days if not weeks to come around to drinkable or at least swimmable. Christmas lunch in the dining room at Waterstreets Hotel was billed in chalk on the counter lunch blackboard as The Festival of Food. There was a ten-shilling surcharge for boarders, for overheads. Rumour had it that some people booked into the hotel just to get a seat at the Christmas lunch. Everybody pitched in to lend Mrs Westie a hand. Dad donated a couple of his best white singlets which Mrs Westie used to hang the puddings, plump and proud, on hooks above the stove. For days on end the magic ingredients hung, nearly bursting out of Dad's singlets like his own tummy, while they secretly blended and matured. Dad loved getting his singlets back because he smelt like Christmas for months.

Jimmy B helped Brasso the cutlery and chains. It wasn't that easy because he had to edge around each dining table, from place to place, careful not to polish too hard lest he break a link and bring the knife or fork even closer to the plate. We broke out the best silver sugar bowls and bread containers with hotel names in running writing on the sides. Some had Waterstreets Hotel but mostly it was the name of another pub, long gone broke, whose best pieces Dad picked up at a Batrouney's auction. It all lent a cosmopolitan feel with the Rose and Thistle ashtrays, the White Horse Hotel milk pourer and the Travellers Arms napkin holders, threaded with scissored quarters of a starched pillowslip fresh from the Modern Steam Laundry. Jimmy B brushed down the old fly paper strips out the back door with the long straw broom before putting them back over each table.

We worked a loophole in the Church law that Harry Flood would have given his eye teeth to think of. St John's Orphanage at Thurgoona had a Midnight Mass on Christmas Eve for all the orphan girls. If you went to Midnight Mass you didn't have to go on Christmas Day. It was like a day off. Even the Mass itself was as close to fun as a church service could get. A black battalion of Sisters Without Mercy from all around the district formed a choir on one side of the small church, challenging the orphans all in white dresses with doilies on their heads on the other.

We Waterstreets sat in the middle, singing our hearts out. It was the battle of the sounds. Katherine Ann's high-pitched *Silent Night* killed them. The Sisters Without Mercy and the orphans were reduced to a chorus for her. They fought back with Hark the Herald Angels Sing, Glory to the Newborn King, which they knew all the words to and the Waterstreets had to just keep the noise up with makeshift words and sound-alike phrases.

By the time of Oh Come All Ye Faithful, Joyful and Triumphant, Oh Come Ye Oh Come Ye to Bethlehem, tears were streaming down in buckets from Dad's eyes and his big white hankie was soaked from the dabbing and nose-blowing. Aunts Hope and Charity were at it, and I blinked a lot trying to keep in touch. I caught up and more. It was the sight of the white orphans, hands joined, looking at the families in the middle of the church, families they had dreamt of having or had lost, and all but bursting out with the wretched unfairness of it all. And God in His Infinite Mercy sat in the Tabernacle at the Altar.

Thoughts of pillowslips filled with presents in the morning kept us going through the Mass. Our bellies tickled inside with the excitement and anticipation. We were crying on the outside but jumping up and down inside, feeling all things at once. Mum would have loved it, and I felt half an orphan myself.

Dad sang You better not shout, You better not cry, You better watch out, I'm telling you why: Santa Claus is coming tonight all the way home in the Holden. I was so exhausted and excited I almost forgot that I didn't believe in Santa Claus any more. Katherine Ann sort of did, but John, Peter and the Hood laid out glasses of milk and arrowroot biscuits for Santa and fresh buffalo grass for the reindeer in front of the new gas heater fitted into the fireplace where the chimney was. Santa would have a lot of trouble getting through the gas jets. Kids will fall for anything.

The trouble with getting older is that your presents get more boring. With Mum away, Dad got us each six pairs of underpants, socks, shirts and a game of Scrabble. Scrabble was fine but everyone wanted to play with their own set and the Hood could hardly speak let alone spell. So we all spent part of the morning playing Scrabble by ourselves, a sort of solo Scrabble like Patience. I think I lost.

The back bar was buzzing with the Christmas spirit. The boarders and anyone booked for lunch were dressed in suits and ties and Cup-day frocks. Ernie Carpenter had a bit of trouble with his tie but Dad fixed it up before they went into the dining room. Jack Davies had lent Uncle one of his suits and shirts for the occasion but they were about twenty sizes too big. Uncle rolled up his trousers and his cuffs. His shirt collar and tie looked like the top of a tight marble bag. J-J-Jack S-S-Shiebs and Captain Jack Saunders (retired) marched into the dining room at three o'clock sharp. It was a tradition that Christmas lunch not be served until then. The back bar was then closed and everyone adjourned to the dining room, where Jimmy B had stuck some handwritten placards with Merry Christmas on the walls with duct tape and hung some streamers and balloons between the fly paper. A small fir tree sprayed with white Santa Snow and with Katherine Ann's dressed doll on top was leaning sideways in soil in a mop bucket in the corner.

The temperature was a couple of degrees beyond boiling point and just perfect for the choice of steaming hot turkey, chicken or mutton with gravy. The Waterstreet family had our own table but everyone got a paper party hat in all sorts of colours. Dad tried to say Grace Before Meals but got it mixed up with the words of confession, so instead of saying Bless us oh Lord for these Thy gifts he said Bless me Father for I have sinned. Everyone said Amen and dug into the thick white slices of yesterday's bread while waiting for the trays of meats and vegies. There was an air of formality at first, in deference to some womenfolk who were dining. But before long the boarders remembered how much they had already drunk and how much they could drink on the house as part of the ten-shilling surcharge and started pulling the initialled corks out of the best of Barney Gehrig's bulk wines and pouring them into middie glasses, right up to the rim. Ernie produced a paper straw from his top pocket and made short work of his first glass.

Dad raided the top shelf in the tap room for a half dozen warm bottles of Pineapple Porphyry Pearl and gave a bottle to each table. Jimmy B said it was bonzer but Dad insisted that Big Jeff Eames open the bar and get a bucket of ice cubes. It's as warm as piss he whispered.

The waitress came from the kitchen to a chorus of ohs and ahs. We tucked into the baked turkey, with sweat dripping on to the laundered bedsheets. The broken chains meant you were closer to a hot meal than you wanted to be and some of the diners went very red and almost passed out. They picked at the meal with their fingers or made sandwiches.

At the end of the first course it was toasting time and Dad tapped the side of his middie glass of Pineapple Porphyry Pearl with a dessert spoon, asking for silence. To absent friends he said, holding the glass to his lips. Mrs Street, the diners murmured at the bottom of their voices with glasses raised and spilling.

The best was yet to come. Most had not eaten much of the main course to leave room for the free drink and Mrs Westie's Christmas pud. The pud was the boarders' Christmas present. The waitress held the tray of bowls over her head and brought it down tantalisingly slowly into view. Piping hot lumps of yellow custard ran like a lava flow down the side of slices of Mrs Westie's black Christmas pudding.

Everyone got a bowl and started digging in with the fork and chain, looking for the coins. The sounds of clinking forks on crockery were soon the only thing that could be heard in the dining room as desperate men and women and children searched among the ruins of raisins, sultanas, almonds, peanuts, cashews and cake for their threepences, sixpences or even pennies. There were none. Nothing. Someone eventually unfurled a wet piece of brown wax paper he found in the pudding. There was a piece in mine. I thought it was just Mrs Westie's absentmindedness. But an unbelieving Jack Davies blurted out the contents of his piece of brown wax paper. I.O.U. Six Pence, signed Bill Waterstreet. Everyone had a piece of paper with some amount written on it. We all looked at Dad in unquiet disappointment. Don't blame me, he shouted. It's Menzies Bloody Credit Squeeze.

By the time everyone drained the last of the Pineapple Porphyry and the Gehrigs, it was time to reopen the back bar for the evening session. A final toast to Mrs Street and they all disappeared out of the dining room. I popped in to see Mrs Westie, who sat on a wooden chair outside the back door with her dress and apron pulled up on her thighs letting the air in between her legs. Can I have some of your pudding to send to Mum in hospital, I asked. Mrs Westie shook her hairnetted greyhaired head. I don't think it would be what the doctor ordered for your dear mother Charles, she said. Why not? She loves your pudding, I told her. A little bit too much I'm afraid, she replied. I use a bottle or two of brandy to make it. I immediately understood that Mum should never have Mrs Westie's pudding again.

The rewiring worked a treat and Mum returned in the New Year with green hand-stitched moccasins for Dad and all the kids. She'd made them in group workshop. I guess the idea was like Father Bongiorno's cure for the rubbing. The devil plays with idle hands. In this case it was the devil inside her head.

So we all made a fuss and turned up for breakfast with our new green felt moccasins with sheepskin insides. The trouble was they were all Dad's size, size 12, and the Hood swam in his, but we all sort of got around like cross country skiers, sliding around Waterstreets in green felt slippers. The lino was never cleaner.

Everyone said I was shooting up. The Waverley College uniform arrived and Mum made me put it on at least once a week. It seemed to shrink just a little every time I put it on.

The rubbing urges got stronger in the summer. I blamed the sun and the Speedo one-piece swimming costumes the girls at the Olympic Pool wore, which stuck like licked envelopes to their skins when they got out of the water. The clothes closet was like a second home. There'd be no clothes closets in Sydney so I was making hay while the sun shone. But I suspected it was like eating. You can't eat like a pig for a week and then not eat. It's got to be three meals a day. So the rubbing followed each meal like clockwork. I was putting the Augustine Attitude into practice.

Mrs Westie added a Summer Salad to the counter lunch menu but hardly anyone ever ordered it. Even on the hottest days they ordered meat pies one veg or steaming haricot chops. The Summer Salad had slices of meats we couldn't sell when they were hot but were kept in the fridge for a time and then called cold cuts. In addition it had lettuce, tomato quarters, beetroot slices, and real Kraft Cheddar cheese cut into cubes the size of dice scattered over. Sometimes the silver paper would give you a shock. Dad thought it was a crying shame they weren't more popular but thanked the good Lord they could be kept for months under tea towels in the fridge. Maybe by next summer people might be used to it.

Mrs Westie tried to get me to eat one of her Summer Salads. She was pretty keen on her handiwork and insisted it would be good for me. Well that about killed any chance I'd eat it. She said to think of the millions starving in China. Name one, I said back. She never pressed me again.

The Albury skyline was getting your more cosmopolitan feel with television aerials sprouting from the roofs of houses like an invasion of giant stick insects. There was another grasshopper plague. Taillight and I went out to North Albury behind St Thomas Aquinas where there were the biggest swarms and ran like boys possessed through the grassy paddocks wearing our diving masks and snorkels to see and breathe while millions of hoppers jumped from the ground and covered us for a leg up. Our gumboots squashed thousands of them like tiny eggs. Crunch. Crunch. Crunch. There was a thirty-foot green cloud of chirping jumping grasshoppers surrounding us so we couldn't see an inch in front of our masks. Some baby ones would get into the top of the snorkel and we'd spit them out in pieces. We had them on the run. I reckoned they wouldn't be game to come back to Albury for a long time after what Taillight and I did to them.

Taillight was braving the streets of Albury in ever increasing squares from his house in his father's Humber. He was soon driving to the Waterworks at Mungabareena with a high school girl, and a blanket in the boot. I didn't go. I wasn't wanted. I would have felt like a shag on a rock anyway.

In mid-January it got so hot the whole family moved all our mattresses on to the verandah above Smollett Street and we all slept there. Mum and Dad snored in stereo. I swear the canvas blinds billowed like the America's Cup challengers when he breathed out. I thought we'd take off. I awoke in a warm puddle of white wet sheets in the middle of the night and tippytoed to the linen closet out the back and changed them. I fretted the rest of the night about boarding school until I fell into a deep exhausted sleep – only to wake in another warm puddle of wet white sheets. Everyone was awake and looking at me going tut-tut-tut. I'd have to stop drinking all liquids immediately. I was a one-boy Waterworks. Not even the Hood wet his bed now. He was four years old. Oh, the shame, the shame.

Time went quickly. I was still awake when the last of the six clocks I'd set the night before went off like a fire alarm. Each clock had been set on the hour in turn when I went to bed. There was a twofold reason. One, naturally, for the bedwetting. The next day Dad was taking me on the *Spirit of Progress* to Sydney and the next night I would be alone in a dormitory of forty boys I'd never met. I needed the practice. I needed a dry run. Second, I wanted to enjoy every second I had left lying on our own verandah, in our own hotel.

Mum herself had starched the new blue shirts and my neck was red raw from the scratching. Dad was very sympathetic. He asked Mum to cut my nails with her scissors. Although there'd been a couple of near misses with the shandies, Mum had pulled herself together and packed one of Dad's biggest suitcases full of my nametagged clothes. Even my hankies had names. She gathered the kids together and we all ate in the dining room together before any of the boarders came down. She wanted to cook what she described as a hearty breakfast. It was so early that the *Border* hadn't been delivered and Dad had to read yesterday evening's Sydney paper. He wore one of his clothes closet suits, which made me a little uneasy. I'm glad suits can't see. The Hood slept with his head on the table. Mum served up burnt bacon and eggs. Tomato sauce was invented for Mum's cooking. It was lucky she was a mum because she wouldn't make a living as a cook. After the hearty breakfast I went upstairs to check I had everything. Comb. Wallet. Coins. Hankie. Holy Card. Rosary Beads. Miraculous Medal. St Christopher Medal for Travellers. Then I checked my other pocket. Prince Valiant comic. Pen. Crossword puzzle. Marbles. Choo-Choo bar. And the fluoride tablets Mum bought for all of us. John, Peter and the Hood helped me lug the suit-case, one clunky step at a time, down the back stairs and bundle it into the open boot. Mum had written my name and Waverley College Birrell Street Syd-ney on the manila-coloured card on a string around the handle. We were set. Dad started the car and told me to run upstairs and say goodbye to your mother.

She was sitting on the footstool under the Green Indonesian Woman in the lounge upstairs. She had her head in her hands sobbing quietly. I stopped dead in my tracks. She looked up with grey black streaks of tears running down her face and into her mouth. Her pale, pale blue eyes looked straight into mine and glowed like the sky. I love you Charlie, I don't want you to go. Tears kept coming. I stood still. Please don't go. I'll miss you so much. Her head fell forward into the cup of her hands.

She had never cried in front of me. Ever. Not ever. Not even in her worst times. Never for herself. Now she was crying for me. I clutched her head and hands in my arms and nestled her on my chest and put my face into her pitch black hair and cried too. I love you too Mum. But I've got to go or we'll miss the train. I backed out of the lounge looking at my handprints on Mum's face. From then on we would grow closer and closer apart.

I'd said my goodbyes the day before to Nana, Auntie Faith and Tom, Auntie Charity and Auntie Hope. Taillight said see ya last Saturday before taking Diana Duckworth for a spin in the Super Snipe, probably to the Waterworks with the blanket in the boot.

The railway station was fifty yards up Smollett Street but Dad insisted on loading us in the Holden and we arrived there in three seconds flat with an almost full load of Waterstreets and a huge Globite suitcase. You could have knocked me down with a feather when I saw all the Jacks and Uncle warming themselves around the gas heater with a half-gallon of white wine in the railway waiting room. I rushed in and shook their hands quickly. They hadn't made the platform but they had made the effort. Although Albury Railway Station platform is the longest in the Southern Hemisphere bar a couple in South America and South Africa we still didn't manage to reach the last carriage of the train known as the *Spirit of Progress* as it pulled away in a cloud of black and blue smoke.

Into the car, hollered Dad, we'll catch it up the road. I sat in the front with the Hood on my lap.

The *Spirit of Progress* came into view just after we went through Table Top at 100 miles an hour. The Hume Highway runs alongside the tracks for about ten miles and by Gerogery West we were a good twenty car lengths in front. Dad sang *It's a Long Way to Tipperary* in time with the wheels of the train. The Holden crossed the railroad tracks at Gerogery with seconds to spare before the mighty steel-blue steam engine hauling the *Spirit of Progress* came to a screeching stop. Dad put the suitcase on the shelf above my seat. He hugged me tightly. On the floor were two heated iron bricks to keep your feet warm. I had a window seat so I stuck my head out and waved furiously until my eyes ran with coal dust. I'm sure it was the coal dust.

Strangely, all the way to Sydney I didn't think about where I was going but where I'd been, who I had been with and what it all meant. The *Spirit of Progress* became my train of thought. The sound of the wheels on the tracks and the endless flight of telegraph poles out the window sort of hypnotised me. It was like Ursula was using her powers in reverse, predicting the past. Everyone came into clear view. All the Jacks and Uncle circled around the gas heater rubbing their hands together for warmth in the middle of a summer heatwave, passing the jug from mouth to mouth with a quick wipe of the rim with a sleeve. Hearts of gold but heads of

275

lead. I loved them all right, but they had fallen victim to the powers of negative thinking. Their lives decayed by the drink.

The Unchristian Brothers flailing away furiously with Uncle Bob's leather straps on outstretched hands and bent-over bottoms of innocent and not so innocent boys. Giving each other short back and side haircuts every second weekend. I guess the strap and the haircut were as close as they got to human physical contact, so they made the most of them.

I even felt sorry for the Sisters Without Mercy. They were all married to the same one man, Jesus Christ, the biggest bigamist of them all, and spent their whole life waiting for him to show up.

I am by Bill out of Kath. In equal parts. For many years I wanted to be mostly Bill and just a little bit Kath, but in the lounge under the eyes of the Green Indonesian Woman I was my mother's son. She made me. Dad is a big man but Mum is the measure of him. I can feel the heart-shaped hole in my chest finally filling up.

I am leaving Katherine Ann, John, Peter and the Hood to fill my green felt moccasins. They have each other, and that piece of me that sleeps forever in room 17, above the green cement beer garden.

Taillight was the elder brother I never had all my life. He hardly had any time for me this last summer. He was drifting away from me to his own life. Not with Diana Duckworth I hoped. He didn't even come to the train station. But Taillight was still part of me. Always will be. We were going to grow further and further together.

Faith, Hope and Charity begin and end at home, in Albury. Mayor Bunton, Nature's Gentleman, would rule with his whim of steel for all time. All my teeth would fall out of my head but I could never blame Albury. In time everything decays. That's the way of the world. Why should Albury be any different? The referendum result was a tribute to the powers of negative thinking. It is so much easier to say No.

Now I was facing Sydney in my cabin seat and my back was turned on Albury. It was time to say Yes. Negative thinking kept everybody down. The time had come to believe in the positive power of negative thinking. You think of something bad, something that keeps you down; you concentrate on it and then you turn it around. If you can change the bad stuff, you can change anything. That's the positive power of negative thinking.

I will not wet my bed ever, ever, ever again.

Acknowledgements

The 1958 map of Albury on the inside front and back cover is reproduced courtesy of the NRMA P/L.

The quotation from *The Prodigal Son*, published in *Australian Letters*, 1958, © Patrick White, is reproduced courtesy of Barbara Mobbs.

Page 65: Lines quoted from 'A White Sport Coat (And A Pink Carnation)', words and music by Marty Robbins, © 1957 renewed 1985 Mariposa Music, USA, Acuff-Rose Music Limited, London W1, used by permission of Music Sales Ltd. All rights reserved. International copyright secured.

The lines quoted on page 91 are from 'The Charge of the Light Brigade' by Alfred, Lord Tennyson.

The lines quoted on page 119 are from 'Sink the Bismarck' (J. Horton/T. Franks), © 1960 Pastor Music Co. Used by permission of EMI Music